Cultivating Native Plants for Pollinators

To tomorrow,
with each of us paving the way!

Cultivating Native Plants for Pollinators
Editors: Jeremy Hauck and Sherry Vitolo
Designer: Wendy Reynolds

ISBN 978-1-58011-620-6

The Cataloging-in-Publication Data is on file with the Library of Congress.

To learn more about the other great books from Fox Chapel Publishing, or to find a retailer near you, call toll-free at 800-457-9112 or visit us at www.FoxChapelPublishing.com.

We are always looking for talented authors. To submit an idea, please send a brief inquiry to acquisitions@foxchapelpublishing.com.

Or write to:
903 Square Street
Mount Joy, PA 17552,

Printed in China
First Printing

Cultivating Native Plants for Pollinators

A Comprehensive Guide to Attracting Birds, Bees, and Butterflies

Helen Yoest

Contents

Cultivating dedicated pollinator spaces has the added benefit of creating beautiful spaces we can enjoy, too.

Introduction: Why Nature Could Use Your Help

One is never lonely when enjoying a pollinator habitat. Each day during spring, summer, and fall, I get daily visits in my half-acre garden in the suburbs of Raleigh, North Carolina, from butterflies, hummingbirds, and bees. The wildlife is briefly startled when I first open the door to step outside, but once I'm busy in the garden, they are not bothered by me. If I stand still, I can see and hear life all around me. Butterflies are fluttering, bees are buzzing, and the hummingbirds know when a flower has been refreshed with nectar.

Pollinators—butterflies, hummingbirds, and bees—are critical in The Bee Better Teaching Garden, my garden where I teach others how to support pollinators and about the work that pollinators do. Other pollinators, such as bats, beetles, flies, moths, wasps, and yes, even the common black ant, are also pollinators in my garden and are featured in my teaching, but this book provides in-depth descriptions of the main pollinators (bees) and our most beloved pollinators (hummingbirds and butterflies), along with the plants they prefer. When you create a haven for these pollinators, your care and efforts reap benefits for *all* pollinators, great and small.

With global issues causing habitat loss, such as rapid residential growth, overuse of pesticides and herbicides, agrochemical use, climate change—hurricanes, wildfires, and changes in phenology—where the life cycles of insects no longer align with the flowering or fruiting times of their host plants—it can be difficult not to internalize these heart-wrenching and disturbing headlines, becoming paralyzed and thinking all is lost. However, we can instill effective change by focusing our energy on creating pollinator sanctuaries in our backyards and

A black-chinned hummingbird drinking nectar from a bloom.

A female ruby-throated hummingbird seeking nectar from some scarlet bee balm.

communities. All habitats, whether it's a balcony, container garden, a small lot, or acreage, are essential to the survival of pollinators. Every garden counts!

By choosing to learn from this book, I know you want to do your part in attracting and protecting pollinators and supporting their beneficial effects on the environment. You will make a difference for all wildlife, especially pollinators, even if it is just one pollinator plant at a time.

The book is structured in five parts. First, a chapter about the history and motivations for cultivating gardens, plus the ins and outs of pollination and why it's important, and what we can do to promote it. Then the four core parts:

Chapter 2: Butterflies. Butterflies are grouped into six families. Within each family, there are several genera and species. Covered within this book are four families (Pieridae and Riodinidae were omitted), as noted below. Butterflies seek nectar from plants. Pollination isn't a priority, but by visiting a flower, they will inadvertently brush up against the stamen (male part) and the pistil (female part) of the plant, thereby playing a crucial role in the process of pollination. For butterflies, I've included nectar and specific host plants needed by specific butterfly species to lay eggs.

- Hesperiidae: skipper butterflies
- Lycaenidae: blues, coppers, hairstreaks, and gossamer-winged butterflies
- Nymphalidae: brush-footed butterflies, including monarchs, admirals, and those lovely painted ladies
- Papilionidae: swallowtails, where most have tails on their hindwings, such as the Anise, Eastern Tiger, and pipevine swallowtails

Chapter 3: Hummingbirds. There is only one hummingbird family—Trochilidae—which includes: Anna's, Allen's, black-chinned, broad-tailed, calliope, ruby-throated, and rufous. The hummingbird, like the butterfly, is only seeking nectar from flowers, and when they brush up against the stamen and pistil they aid in pollination by accident.

Chapter 4: Bees. There are seven recognized families of bees worldwide, with the five most common—and the ones covered in this book—being Andrenidae, Apidae, Colletes, Halictidae, and Megachilidae. The family Stenotritidae is found only in Australia, and the family Melittidae

A bumblebee gathering pollen.

is mostly located in Central and South America. Bees seek nectar as their primary source of energy, and it is used to make honey. Bees also seek pollen for essential proteins and other nutrients to feed the developing larvae in the hive. While seeking these vital resources, bees also play a crucial role in pollination, transferring pollen from one flower to another and enabling the plants to reproduce. Flowers, in turn, have evolved various ways to attract bees, including their bright colors, fragrances, and nectar guides (patterns visible in ultraviolet light).

Chapter 5: Native Plant Profiles. This book blends the sciences of ornithology, entomology, and botany, and in discussing plants and animals, the scientific names cannot be avoided. I have kept references to these scientific names as simple as possible, however. Just know that the plant profiles are listed by genus and species. If you want to add a native aster to your garden (and of course you do), look under the Aster pages to see if one is native to you. Additionally, within the pollinator plant profiles, I have also designated plant profiles according to their North American hardiness zones. If a listed plant is not native in your region, but will thrive in your hardiness zone, it is a distribution plant. You can also consider adding those to your garden. I'll tell you about the following native plant genuses in chapter 5:

- Agastache
- Asters
- Columbine
- Coreopsis
- Crossvine
- Cup Plants
- Joe-Pye Weed
- Lobelia
- Lupines
- Monarda
- Mountain Mint
- Penstemon
- Phlox
- Rudbeckia
- Salvias
- Solidago
- Verbena

In this book, you will learn how to help pollinators by planting the plants they require. This book covers many of the host and nectar plants for butterflies, nectar plants for hummingbirds, and the best nectar and pollen plants for our native bees. For example, I write about various species of Joe-Pye weed, including *Eutrochium fistulosum*. This plant is hollow stemmed, an important nesting site for various solitary native bees—a bonus beyond nectar and pollen. And, while honeybees are not native to North America, and their floral preferences aren't necessarily native either, honeybees are so vital to our pollinator habitats that I would be remiss in leaving them out.

The pollinators will find you. Plant the plants, hang the hummingbird nectar feeder, and add nesting sites for solitary bees. You'll be amazed. Take it one step at a time, but please do take that step, and congratulations on being part of a movement of pollinator habitat creators!

Bignonia capreolata, commonly known as the crossvine.

CHAPTER 1

Getting Started

Initially, our ancestors gardened for food. As interest in ornamental gardening grew, certain plants became fashionable among those who could afford it. That was especially true during the during the Dutch Golden Age. During the "Tulipomania" of the 1630s, a single tulip bulb could cost as much as a house.

I can imagine the showiness of new colors and color combinations of tulip petals, once opened on frigid fields for the first time, warming hearts. The snowdrops, too, arrive at a time when tiny treasures emerge from the snow. (About 40 years ago, gardeners became fascinated with snowdrops—an obsession dubbed "Galanthomania," named after the genus Galanthus.) For some, discovering a snowdrop's yellow spathe or an unusual placement of a green dot excites the senses.

My excitement for gardening, however, comes from different pleasures. I plant for pollinators, including umbel-shaped inflorescences for butterflies to alight

A small copper butterfly (*Lycaena phlaeas*), nectaring on knapweed flowers in July.

on, tubular-shaped flowers for hummingbirds to delight in, and I admire the creative ways native bees seek nectar. I also enjoy watching the honeybee sip nectar and collect pollen to provide for their brood and honey lovers around the world. Let us create a new mania—Pollinator Mania!

Rebuilding Habitat Intentionally

In all those decades between tulips in the 17th century and snowdrops in the 20th, other plants and styles became a fascination—ferns, orchids, food, and repeat. Then there were designs, such as formal, cottage, and naturalist gardens; repeat. It seems we are never satisfied. But times have changed. A pollinator garden is more than a style—it's a need for our society to function effectively. We know that pollinator gardening is not a trend, just as living is not a trend, and we would like to see it continue. We want to do our part to help the Earth.

It may take some time, but you will eventually see butterflies, hummingbirds, and bees enjoying your garden. If you are planting a new garden, be patient. Perennial plants take time to mature. Gardening is truly a leisurely lifestyle, not a rabbit race. The expression is:

> *"First year they sleep, second year they creep, third year they leap."*

Our collective efforts can rebuild local wildlife habitats, one pollinator at a time. Once you start with one pollinator, such as bees, and see the results, you can go on to attract more, maybe hummingbirds, then butterflies. Even if you have a formal landscape, there is always room to carve a space for habitat gardening. Most of the suggested plants in this book benefit all three pollinator groups—butterflies, hummingbirds, and bees.

Working in the Garden

Gardening isn't a one-and-done endeavor. Thank goodness—this leaves room for us to grow and learn! Gardening evolves as we develop our understanding of nature. Don't feel overwhelmed, though—starting small is the best way to begin your journey into thoughtful pollinator gardening.

If you've already laid the groundwork for creating a garden, this book will guide you in adding the best plants to attract butterflies, hummingbirds, and bees. Each species has specific needs, some very specific, such as the monarch's requirement for a host plant in the milkweed family Asclepiadaceae. Native bees have specific nesting needs, and we can also make nesting sites.

When purchasing plants, I recommend buying three or more of each, to increase the visibility from up above, and as they will be clustered together, less effort is needed for the pollinators to feed.

The Meaning of Earth Day

While the 1960s highlighted social injustices, the 1970s focused on environmental improvement. The Clean Air Act was initially passed in 1963, but the 1970 amendments significantly improved it.

In 1970, I was a curious and adventurous 14-year-old. I spent my daylight hours discovering new adventures in nature and the environment. I knew I would grow up working toward bettering the environment, and I did—I went on to become an air pollution engineer, researching and trialing test methods to measure emissions from industrial smokestacks, considered "stationary source emissions."

Even today, as a writer specializing in sustainable gardening, wildlife habitats, and the plants that benefit pollinators, I strive to inspire others to take up the cause. April 22, 1970, was the first Earth Day; I remember it well. I celebrated by visiting my beloved field across the street, barefoot and running through acres of flatland, filled with cattails providing food, shelter, and nesting sites for various wildlife. A small Chesapeake Bay tributary was on the far side of the field; thus, between the two, I was offered an opportunity for endless fascinations. (Those cattails were likely the southern cattail, *Typha domingensis*.) Today, that area is a ball field.

The Clean Water Act was passed in 1972, establishing a nationwide approach to protecting water quality and regulating the discharge of pollutants. (My husband is an industrial wastewater

As temperatures warm, monarch butterflies become a bit more active. This provided a surreal experience for Nathalie Beauchamp during a visit to the monarch butterfly overwintering site in Mexico.

engineer; like-minded individuals tend to gravitate toward one another: we got married in 1988.)

In the winter of 1975, Dr. Fred Urquhart's scientific team discovered the monarch overwintering site for those migrating monarchs east of the Rockies. Not only did we learn about this wintering site, but we also gained insight into its significance for the people of Mexico. The Day of the Dead is celebrated on November 1 and 2. Around this time, the monarch butterfly returns to its wintering site in Mexico, so the locals have long associated the monarch butterfly with the souls of the deceased.

Enemies of Pollinators: Herbicides

Herbicide use poses a threat to pollinators and the broader web of life, which includes us. A popular herbicide is glyphosate. When used safely, following label instructions, the EPA has found no risks of concern to human health. The EPA has also found that glyphosate is unlikely to be a human carcinogen. But are homeowners using glyphosate properly?

Glyphosate Use in the Habitat Garden

Glyphosate has strict requirements for its use. If you use glyphosate, are you following a strict application protocol? In my home garden, I don't use glyphosate. It is just me and my garden hoe. However, if you choose to use glyphosate, follow the glyphosate application protocol.

- Always read and follow label instructions.
- Apply on a calm, dry day with temperatures above 60°F.
- Spray directly onto the leaves of target weeds.
- Avoid contact with desirable plants.
- Wear protective gear such as gloves and eye protection.
- Ensure the treated area is completely dry before allowing people or pets access.

Lawns are essentially a desert for pollinators.

Clear cutting damages important habitats.

Clients often ask me, when mixing concentrated glyphosate with water, is adding more active ingredients better? (A term I frequently hear is "sweetening the pot.") No, it isn't, I tell them.

In agriculture, certain crop seeds are genetically modified for use with glyphosate. This means the genetically modified seeds can now receive this herbicide spray to rid weeds, leaving the modified crops untouched. These crops include alfalfa, canola, corn, cotton, sorghum, soybeans, and sugar beets, and maybe more.

The farmlands that use these genetically modified seeds are creating pollinator deserts once herbicide is applied, wiping out host plants and the pollinators that need them for survival. The use of glyphosate-ready genetically modified crops leads to the killing of milkweeds from fields, the monarch butterfly's only host plant, contributing to the monarch's decline.

Enemies of Pollinators: Habitat Loss and Climate Change

Urbanization and ever-increasing infrastructure development have significantly impacted our environment, leading to the loss of wildlife habitats. Pollinators cannot find enough food or the right food quality, high in nectar and pollen, for survival. With increased rainfall, droughts, hurricanes, wildfires, and other natural disasters, climate change is furthermore threatening the habitats of pollinators, making it difficult for them to survive. Migratory pollinators need consistent sources of pollen and nectar; if there are gaps between one flowering area and another, pollinators may starve. We need to build a pollinator highway. Each of us can help make that happen.

Plan for Food in Every Season

Phenology is the study of cyclic and seasonal natural phenomena. Phenology, in part, is about the timing of a pollinator's arrival and if or when their preferred plants are available. We are starting to see shifts in bloom times and the arrival of pollinators. So far, the bloom cycles in my garden have been long enough to accommodate pollinators, but will they always be in sync as the weather warms earlier? With plants blooming earlier, will the columbine still bloom when the hummingbirds arrive from their long migration?

At her best, nature has built-in mechanisms to help pollinators thrive, with plants evolving to have differing flowering times throughout the year so that there is decreased competition for pollen and nectar. Providing pollinating plants that flower throughout the seasons is essential to ensure a continuous food supply and nesting materials for various pollinators. Let's get into the seasons and how we can work with them now.

Spring

Pollinators require early-blooming plants to provide food after hibernation or northern migrations. Bulbs, spring ephemerals, and spring-flowering fruit trees pollinate during this time. In my home garden, I have something in bloom every month of the year. Finding a bumblebee emerging from a winter slumber to sup on nectar from any available flowering plants is not unusual.

Summer

The peak of our summer's flowering season is also the peak of pollinator populations. I enjoy nothing more than having my morning coffee (thank you, bees, for pollinating the coffee plants) on my back covered porch and watching the pollinators feed. I can always count on the hummingbirds first thing in the morning since they know to revisit the nectar flowers they drained the day before. I often find bumblebees sleeping on their nectar source. Butterflies are cold-blooded and must wait until it's warm enough, later in

A peak summertime view of Raleigh's Prairie Ridge Ecostation, the outdoor extension of the North Carolina Museum of Natural Sciences.

Stick piles and leaf litter provide overwinter sheltering spaces for pollinators.

the day, to fly. I'll find butterflies basking in the sun on the stone steps before they can take flight, waiting to warm their flight muscles; most butterfly flight activity occurs when temperatures are between 70°F and 85°F.

Fall

My experience speaking with gardeners has been that fall gardening gives way to football, school, soccer, and other family events, and autumn gardening is often forgotten. However, planting fall-blooming flowers is just as important as having summer-flowering delights. Even if you are too busy to tend an elaborate garden, aim to plant for pollinators in a low-maintenance, sustainable way. A fall habitat provides late-blooming flowers for the many pollinators that need fuel before bee hibernation and for the southern migrations, such as monarchs and hummingbirds.

Winter

If you lack winter-flowering plants, there are still ways to help the pollinators. For one, leave decaying plants alone. If you prefer a tidier space, cut the stems back, leaving a height of six to eight inches. These stems can shelter or host pollinating insects as they overwinter. Leave a stick pile, leaf litter, and uncovered north-facing soil so the queen bumblebee can dig her hole to hibernate. Nesting sites become fragmented through housing development, road construction, and farming, and if you maintain a pristine garden devoid of these natural nesting grounds, you will contribute to the losses. We can do our part by providing pollinator habitats within reach of food and clean, shallow water sources.

Pollination Basics

Pollination is what makes our ecosystem strong and healthy. Those fruits and treats you love—almonds, coffee, apples, avocados, blackberries, blueberries, cherries, chocolate, cranberries, eggplant, figs, grapes, lemons, limes, oranges, peaches, pears, plums, raspberries, and so many more—are made possible by pollination. Personally, I would be lost without my morning cuppa coffee!

For pollination to occur, several steps need to take place. First, pollinators need to be lured in by a flower's generous offerings of color, smell, or nectar. While feeding and visiting a garden, these pollinators brush against pollen and carry it with them as they move from flower to flower. Next, this pollen needs to travel from the flower's male part, called the anther, to the flower's female part, called the stigma. This fertilization process later yields the fruits and seeds that both wildlife and our society need to function. Bees are the masters at this and are essential pollinators. Butterflies and hummingbirds are only seeking nectar, so I think of them as accidental pollinators, but they do their part.

Blueberries, cranberries, eggplants, peppers, potatoes, and tomatoes house their pollen in poricidal anthers—tube-shaped anthers that open small pores to release pollen. These anthers are inside long, narrow flowers. To release the pollen, bees will perform what's referred to as buzz pollination—a method of pollination where bees use vibrations to release pollen from flowers. Bees must shake the anthers to release the pollen. They accomplish this by placing their thorax close to the anthers and contracting their flight muscles at about 400 hertz (400 cycles per second).

About 8 percent of fall-flowering plants require buzz pollination. Bumblebees, mining bees, and sweat bees are effective pollinators of these crops. In addition, even plants with non-poricidal anthers, such as pumpkins and squash, benefit from sonication.

The Big Four Factors for a Habitat Garden

There are four major factors to consider when creating a garden intended to be a habitat for pollinators. These factors are the elements pollinators require to survive and thrive.

1: Food for Pollinators

The more food sources you have, the greater the variety of pollinators you'll attract. The highest-quality food sources that you can use are regionally native plants, which can typically support ten to fifty times more local pollinators than non-native plants. You can also supplement the naturally occurring food for hummingbirds with nectar feeders and manmade houses, and hollow-stemmed plants for bee nesting sites.

Remember to think about more than just the summer growing season. Pollinators need nectar early in the spring, throughout the summer, and especially into the fall. Choosing plants that bloom at different times will help create a bright and colorful garden that benefits both you and pollinators.

Also, food needs should be considered at different life cycle stages for pollinators. For example, the butterfly larvae feed on specific host plants (depending on the type of butterfly). At the same time, adults sip the nectar of most flowers with an umbel shape, providing them with a landing pad for butterflies to alight.

2: Water Sources in the Garden

Water is essential for drinking and bathing, and a clean, reliable water source is crucial for creating a healthy habitat. Providing water can be as simple as adding a birdbath. To attract a greater variety of pollinators, add water in multiple locations throughout your garden, at varying heights. It's essential to provide water year-round, even in the winter and especially during times of drought. Locate the water source with an easy view to make it entertaining for the gardener and also to keep an eye on to see when refreshing is needed.

Bees drinking from a birdbath. Birdbaths are great multipurpose additions to any garden.

Wax mrytle provides shelter for pollinators.

Solitary bees need hollow spaces for nesting.

3: Cover

Pollinators need cover to protect themselves against the elements and predators. Having a place to escape the threat of pending danger will attract more pollinators to your garden. Various plants, ranging in size, height, and density, including trees, shrubs, perennials, annuals, vines, and ornamental grasses, can provide ample cover and increase your success in attracting pollinators

4: Places to Raise Their Young

Sources of cover also provide a safe place for your pollinator friends to reproduce and nurture their young. Dense shrubbery and understory trees offer secure areas for hummingbirds to nest in a backyard. Leave hollow-stemmed stalks for native bees as nesting sites or build one of your own (see pages 110–11).

Mulch and Its Benefits

Sustainable gardening practices will also benefit your pollinator habitat. Control non-native and invasive species and reduce or eliminate the use of pesticides, herbicides, and fungicides.

Mulching around plants helps by suppressing weeds, retaining moisture, controlling soil erosion, winter heaving, and slowly breaking down to add natural fertilizer. Additionally, when rain seeps through the mulch in your garden, the mulch improves water quality by filtering out pollutants.

Turning Lawns into Pollinator-Friendly Habitats

Lush green grass has been an American staple since the end of World War II. My parents had a lawn, and my job was to mow it weekly, removing any "evil dandelions" (their words, not mine), and use an edger on wheels to keep the lawn edges nice and crisp. Neglecting those chores would lead the neighbors to gossip about our unkempt yard. The one worthy plant growing in my parents' lawn was a green glade of grass.

During the mid-century in the United States, specifically beginning after World War II, veterans and the rising middle class found affordable housing and a plot of soil to sow grass; land, albeit small, to grow their grassy plain. My parents were among them.

During World War II, significant product developments were made to enhance the suburban homes and lawns, and those products were gaining popularity. Clover could be eliminated, allowing only blades of grass to sprout, and its role in the ecosystem filled by commercial products. Those products included fertilizers, pesticides, and other amendments. My parents followed this modern approach. Without clover's nitrogen-fixing function, grass lawns deplete soil nutrients, so fertilizers, particularly nitrogen, needed to be added.

A cycle was begun. Supplementing with nitrogen and overusing pesticides, herbicides, and fungicides pollutes groundwater and surface waters through runoff, harming wildlife. Modern Americans use more than 80 million pounds of pesticides on their lawns and gardens every year.

Shredded grass and dried leaves are perfect for creating mulch beds.

There is a better way—a pollinator lawn. Pollinator lawns are a tight mix of grasses and low-growing pollinator plants such as clover. They are all green, like traditional lawn grasses, but offer high-quality nutrition to pollinators and feed the soil instead of functioning as a biological desert.

Changing your lawn is not an all-or-nothing proposition. Grass lawns, to many, invoke deep-seated feelings, and you don't need to stoke discontent to achieve your goal of re-greening the environment around you—you can start small by adding beneficial plants and reducing the size of the grass lawn, a bit at a time.

The Magic of Clover

Clover works just as well above ground as it does below. Pollinators feed on clover blooms, and clover is considered North America's most critical group of honeybee plants. There are several species of clover, *Trifolium* spp., and all are good fodder plants, cover crops, and green manure.

As a legume, clover fixes nitrogen, enriching the soil and improving lawn growth. Mow the lawn weekly; no supplements needed. Given its environmentally friendly and low-maintenance nature, although

Clover lawns are much more environmentally friendly than traditional lawn deserts.

not native, clover is undoubtedly a great option as a sustainable lawn replacement.

In the protected garden I'm conserving in Raleigh, North Carolina, the Joslin Garden, fescue grass is mixed with white Dutch clover, *Trillium repens*. We also added Tommies, *Crocus tommasinianus*, for early spring color and nectar. These crocuses will finish blooming before the first mowing is required.

In addition to attracting a wide variety of bee species, including the endangered rusty-patched bumblebee, *Bombus affinis*, Dutch clover also attracts wasps and butterflies.

Particularly, clover is a host plant for the southern dogface, *Zerene cesonia*, gray hairstreak, *Strymon melinus*, greenish blue, *Plebejus saepiolus*, Shasta blue, *P. shasta*, eastern tailed-blue, *Cupido comyntas*, as well as several sulfur butterflies—the orange sulfur, *Colias eurytheme*, clouded sulfur, *C. philodice*, and Queen Alexander's sulfur, *C. Alexandra*.

A bumblebee pollinating a pattypan squash.

Let Nature Help You

Bagging grass clippings should be a thing of the past. Grass clippings feed your soil. Letting grass clippings fall where they're cut naturally and safely fertilizes the lawn, providing up to around 25% of the nitrogen needed to thrive. In addition, a pollinator lawn will require less water and maintenance than traditional grass lawns, yet still provide a green oasis for picnics, relaxation, and yard games.

By letting clover and other pollinating plants, formerly known as weeds, gain traction in your lawn, you'll gain time in your busy life by mowing less. Other areas ideal for a pollinator lawn include sidewalk strips, steep slopes, and areas that are generally ignored. Allowing dandelions, clover, and other "weeds" to bloom—and not poisoning or whacking them back—provides a source of pollen and nectar to feed the pollinators.

Pollinator-Friendly Lawn Plants

Clovers and dandelions aren't the only pollinator plants that benefit bees and butterflies. If you cannot find premixed blends of grass with pollinator plant seeds, add any or all of the following to your grassy areas.

- Bird's-foot trefoil, *Lotus corniculantus*, hardiness zones 4 to 9, benefiting bees and butterflies
- Bluets, *Houstonia longifolia*, hardiness zones 3 to 8, benefiting bees and butterflies, and is the larval host plant for the spotted thyri moth, *Thyris maculata*.
- Common blue violet, *Viola sororia*, hardiness zones 3 to 9, benefiting flies, bees, and butterflies, particularly as a larval host for various fritillaries—the Aphrodite fritillary, *Speyeria aphrodite*; great spangled fritillary, *Speyeria cybele*; meadow fritillary, *Boloria bellona*; silver-bordered fritillary, *Boloria selene*; and variegated fritillary, *Euptoieta claudia*.
- Pussytoes, *Antennaria plantaginifolia*, hardiness zones 3 to 8, benefiting bees and butterflies, particularly as a larval host for the American painted lady, *Vanessa virginiensis*.
- Selfheal, Prunella vulgaris, hardiness zones 4 to 9, benefiting bumblebees, *Bombus* spp., and honeybees, *Apis mellifera*. Plus, the larval host plant for the clouded yellow sulfur butterfly, *Colias croceus*.
- Thyme, *Thymus* spp., hardiness zones 4 to 9, benefiting bumblebees and honeybees. The tiny sweat bee, *Augochlora pura*, is attracted by the aroma of creeping thyme, *Thymus serphyllum*, which has small flowers.
- Virginia strawberry, *Fragaria virginiana*. hardiness zones 4 to 9, benefiting moths, butterflies, and it's the larval host plant for the gray hairstreak butterfly, *strymon melinus*, and attracting over 50 bird species to feed on these native strawberries.
- Virginia spring beauty, *Claytonia virginica*. Hardiness zone—3 to 9, benefiting bees and. Other insects are larval host plants for the spring beauty miner bees, *Andrena erigeniae*. These bees lay their eggs inside their underground nest, on pollen balls from the spring beauty flowers.

Bird's foot trefoil is a beautiful plant that is beneficial to bees and butterflies.

CHAPTER

2

Butterflies

Seeing a butterfly certainly evokes a childlike wonder at any age. But putting aside from their beauty and magical nature for a moment, we need a wake-up call. Butterflies are in peril and being lost at a catastrophic rate. As individuals, each gardener can help make a difference. As the number of pollinator habitats grows and we become a collective, we can serve as educators, with our gardens serving as whiteboards, to share with others how to create pollinator habitats most beneficial to butterflies.

Although the losses vary from year to year, the decline is evident: on average, there has been a 22 percent decline in butterflies since 2020. Five butterflies have become extinct in the US since 1950; 29 are endangered, and six are threatened.

With 17,500 butterfly species worldwide and about 750 species in the US and Canada, you can imagine how impossible it would be to cover all the butterflies north of Mexico. Instead, this book covers the most common butterflies and their essential host plants. This book will help you create a butterfly-friendly habitat best suited for your environment and your butterflies' needs.

You may only want to include plants native to your region or consider adding distribution plants—those plants not native to your region but still in your hardiness zone—as long as their cultural requirements are met.

For example, beardtongue, *Penstemon grandiflorus*, is native to the Great Plains and parts of the Midwest. It lives within hardiness zones 3 to 8, so I can grow it in my Raleigh pollinator garden as a distribution plant. It performs beautifully, luring in the pollinators!

There are six butterfly families native to the US and Canada—Hesperiidae (skippers), Nymphalidae (brush-footed), Riodinidae (metal marks), Lycaenidae (gossamer-winged), Papilionidae (swallowtails), and Pieridae (sulfurs and whites). This book features four of the six butterfly families (all of the above minus Riodinidae and Pieridae) and the most common butterflies within each of the featured families. Those omitted included whites and sulfur butterflies, which mainly feed on crops and are considered nuisances by many vegetable gardeners. Also, whites are non-native, having been accidentally introduced from Europe to the US in the 1860s. Also omitted are metal marks, since they are mostly found in Central and South America.

Pay attention to the ways butterflies overwinter. Think twice before clear-cutting your summer garden!

A checkerspot butterfly in California.

Puddling Sites for Butterflies

There is such enjoyment in watching a butterfly gracefully move from one flower to another, stopping to sip nectar. But is nectar enough? Nectar is pure sugar water; the butterfly's diet also requires salt and other minerals to be complete.

Puddling, or mudding, is a behavior many butterflies engage in, particularly male butterflies. Puddling sites can be found in various locations, including in dung, mud, rotting fruit, plants, and even animal carcasses. Puddling is characterized by a butterfly actively seeking out a moist surface where they use their long, straw-like tongue, called a proboscis, to suck up the salts, minerals, and amino acid–dense fluids. Male butterflies stores these nutrients in their sperm. When the time comes to mate, the male passes these nutrients from his spermatophore, a nuptial gift, to the female. The female now possesses an extra boost, which she then passes to her eggs.

Eggs receiving these nutrient gifts have a greater chance of survival than those that do not. If a male butterfly cannot find a moist site, he will regurgitate onto the soil and then drink it to gain nutrients that dissolve in the saliva.

In my home garden, I made a managed puddling site within a birdbath. I used regular play sand with added nutrients, consisting of three parts sand and one part a nutrient base. These nutrients came from manure from my chickens—if that doesn't sound appealing, or if you don't have livestock, off-the-shelf organic fertilizers are suitable alternatives. Any organic fertilizers will contain the minerals and electrolytes butterflies require. As a shallow source, it will dry out quickly. Keep the site moist. Trays of past-prime fruit or a patch of soil, free of plants and mulch, also work.

Your puddling site may attract bees, but since my puddling site is located within the mixed border, full of pollinator plants that butterflies, hummingbirds, and bees enjoy, it's the perfect location to bring in the pollinators, and it looks natural. Tiger swallowtails are known puddlers, but don't be surprised if you see some sulfurs or even a cabbage white or two.

Have you ever had a butterfly land on your skin and start licking you? It was just using you for your sweat. Some butterflies even take a liking to blood and tears. Puddling sites are easy to create and don't require much space.

A group of butterflies puddling in the sun.

Swallowtails

Family: Papilionidae; Subfamilies: Baroniinae, Parnassiinae, and Papilioninae

Description: The Papilionidae swallowtail family includes large, lovely insects, consisting of anise, eastern black, giant, palamedes, pipevine, spicebush, tiger, two-tailed tiger, and zebra butterflies. Swallowtails are known for their large size and prominent tails, which extend from their hindwings. These tails serve as a safety device, providing a prominent area for predators, such as birds, to try to grab hold of when feeding, breaking off, and protecting the swallowtail's tender bodies. Swallowtails have other safety devices, such as big eyespots on their wings, and rank-smelling caterpillar horns, called osmeteria, to frighten predators. Pipevine swallowtail caterpillars ingest toxins from the Dutchman's pipe vine, *Aristolochia* spp., and when eaten, their taste becomes unappealing to predators.

Zebra Swallowtails lay their eggs on the leaves of pawpaw trees.

Anise Swallowtail

Papilio zelicaon

Description: The population trend is considered relatively stable in many areas, although there have been some declines in certain regions. Their preferred habitats include open areas such as fields, gardens, hilltops, lowlands with open canopies, mountains, roadsides, and vacant lots. They typically have only one brood from April to July, although in warmer locations, they can have up to four broods per year. The anise swallowtail can be confused with the eastern tiger swallowtail. Both are large butterflies with yellow and black coloring. Upon closer examination, distinct differences are apparent. The anise swallowtail is smaller, with more black markings, and features a broad yellow band across the center of the forewing and yellow spots along the wing edges. The wingspan ranges from 2¾ to 3½ inches (7 to 9 cm). Their six legs, including their antennae, are covered in setae (sensory hairs). They have a short black tail that extends from the posterior margin of each of their hindwings, giving the appearance of having a forked tail. They are primarily yellow, with broad yellow bands on their hindwings and forewings extending to their wings' bases.

The anise swallowtail butterfly features a strong yellow color.

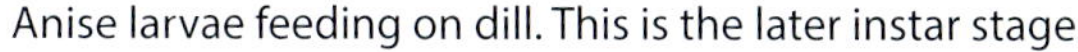
Anise larvae feeding on dill. This is the later instar stage.

An earlier green anise butterfly chrysalis.

Dimorphism: Sexual no, seasonal yes. The spring form typically is small, pale, and heavily marked with blue, and features narrow dark borders on all wings. The summer form is larger, having a richer yellow color, broader black borders, and little or no blue in males.

Generations: Varies by location—one generation in high altitudes, up to four per year at sea level

Lifespan: 6–14 days

Eggs: laid singly on host plant leaves and flowers. They are spherical and pale yellow. As the egg matures, a red ring develops around the middle.

Larvae: early instars are mostly black with white stripes or spots, while later instars become green with black and yellow stripes. They also have Y-shaped glands located behind their heads, which emit a foul odor in response to the threat of predators.

Number of instars: 5

Chrysalis: Green at first, then slowly turns brown as butterflies develop within the pupa. This stage lasts around 4 weeks.

Range: South into Mexico; west of the Rockies, to the Pacific Coast; north into Canada

Larval host plants: Plants in the Apiaceae family, consisting of carrot tops, dill, fennel, water hemlock, and water dropwort

Nectar sources: Asters, coreopsis, mints, oregano, scabiosa, verbenas

Migration or overwintering: Non-migratory; overwinters as chrysalids

Fun fact: When disturbed, the larvae can extend orange, foul-smelling stinkhorns called osmeteria from behind their head to ward off would be predators.

Eastern Black Swallowtail

Papilio polyxenes asterius

Description: The population trend of the eastern black swallowtail is considered generally stable. Their preferred habitats include fields, flatwoods, gardens, pine savannas, roadsides, uplands, weedy areas, and wet prairies. Eastern black swallowtails have two broods in the north and at least three broods in the south, with their flights around mid-May to early July and mid-July to mid-September. Their flight is fast and agile. Adult butterflies are 3 to 4½ inches (8 to 10 cm) with a black upper surface of the wings, with two rows of yellow spots. There is a red spot with a black pupil (bullseye) on the inner hind margin of the hindwings and an isolated yellow spot on the costa (the leading edge) of the forewings. The undersides of the forewings have two rows of pale-yellow spots, while the hindwings have rows of bright orange spots separated by powdery blue areas. Females are typically larger than males. The eyespots on the dorsal side are large and bright in males and smaller and lighter in females. Additionally, the area between the rows of spots on the hindwings of females is a powdery iridescent blue, while this area is much less prominent in males.

An eastern black swallowtail nectaring.

Dimorphism: Sexual yes, seasonal no

Generations: 2 to 3, depending on region

Lifespan: Adult butterflies can live from two weeks to a month.

Eggs: Pale yellow. They are laid singly on the host plants' new foliage or flowers. This stage typically lasts between four and nine days.

Larvae: These can grow up to 1½ to 2 inches (4 to 5 cm) long. Young larvae are predominantly black, with a distinctive white saddle. Older larvae are green with black transverse bands and yellow spots. This stage lasts between 10 to 30 days.

Number of instars: 5

Chrysalis: The butterfly pupates in a head-up position, supported by a silk girdle. Pupae of the overwintering generation are brown, but other generations are green with yellow or brown markings. This stage lasts between 9 and 18 days (excluding overwintering time).

Range: East of the Rockies

Larval host plants: Members of the Apiaceae family, including carrots, celery, dill, fennel, parsley, rue, *Zizia aurea*, and Queen Anne's Lace

Nectar sources: Coneflowers, milkweed, Joe-Pye weed, phlox, thistle, verbena, zinnias

Migration or overwintering: Non-migratory, overwinters as chrysalids

Fun fact: As larvae, these butterflies have horn-like organs, called osmeteria, that protrude when disturbed. Larvae use their bright yellow-orange osmeterium to repel potential predators with a chemical deterrent.

A colorful eastern black swallowtail larva.

An eastern black swallowtail chrysalis (and a younger larva nearby).

This larva has its osmeterium extended to repel potential predators.

Eastern Tiger Swallowtail

Papilio glaucus

Description: The population trend of the eastern tiger swallowtail is generally considered stable and they are widespread. Their preferred habitats include fields, deciduous forests, forest edges near water sources, gardens, woodlands, roadsides, and urban parks or woodlands. There are two broods in the north from May to September, and at least three to four broods from February to November in the deep South. They are known to be high fliers. They have wingspans ranging from 3 to 5½ inches (8 to 10 cm).

Both sexes have a prominent orange marginal spot on the upper side of their hindwing, generally larger than the row of pale marginal spots. Male eastern tiger swallowtails are yellow with dark tiger stripes, with limited blue coloring. Females have two forms: one yellow, like the male, or a dark form, black with shadows of dark stripes. Both female forms have blue chevrons and an iridescent blue wash over parts of the interior hindwing. The black form female tiger swallowtail protects itself by mimicking the pipevine swallowtail, *Battus philenor*, which is toxic to many predators. Predators avoid both, even though the female black form of the eastern swallowtail isn't harmful.

A female eastern tiger swallowtail (yellow form) on a carrot flower.

A female eastern tiger swallowtail (black form) on clover.

A male eastern tiger swallowtail on Joy-Pye weed.

An eastern tiger swallowtail caterpillar snacking on a leaf.

An eastern tiger swallowtail chrysalis.

Dimorphism: Sexual yes, seasonal yes, with the ventral side of the forewing of spring individuals having a row of marginal spots that merge into a continuous band

Generations: 1 to 2, depending on region

Lifespan: Adult butterflies live for between 6 and 14 days.

Eggs: Small and spherical-shaped green eggs laid singly on the upper surface of leaves, turning yellowish green with red dots as they mature. This stage lasts between four and ten days.

Larvae: Newly hatched larvae often eat their eggshells. Larvae create "silk mats" to rest on the upper surface of leaves. The larvae are polyphagous as they can feed on the leaves of various woody plants. Young larvae are brown with a white saddle on their abdomen, maturing to a green color. This stage lasts around 8 to 14 days.

Number of instars: 5

Chrysalis: Often pupate on the underside of twigs or dead leaves on the ground. Chrysalids range from off white to dark brown and are often mottled with green or dark brown. They also have two horn-like projections on their head and one on the thorax. They commonly hang from tree trunks, fence posts, and ground litter. This stage lasts between 7 and 11 days (not including overwintering time).

Range: Alaska to the Atlantic Ocean, south to Texas and Florida

Larval host plants: Ashes, birches, tulip tree, wild cherries, willows

Nectar sources: Blazing star, butterfly bush, coneflowers, ironweeds, Joe-Pye weed, lilacs, milkweeds, oregano, zinnias

Migration or overwintering: Non-migratory; they overwinter as chrysalids.

Fun fact: Female butterflies are the heterogametic sex (XY), and males are the homogametic (XX). As such, yellow females give birth to yellow females, and black females give birth to black females, indicating that the gene for color is on the Y chromosome.

Pipevine Swallowtail

Battus philenor

Description: The population trend of pipevine swallowtails is generally stable and they are widespread. Their preferred habitats include gardens, meadows, shrub thickets, open woodlands, and woodland edges. In the north, their flight ranges from March to November, while they can be found year-round in the southern or warmest parts of their region. Their flight is described as quick and choppy, with short flight ranges. The quick flapping of their wings is the most distinctive feature that allows me to identify them easily. Their flight is so unique. Adult butterflies: They have a wingspan ranging from 2¾ to 5 inches (7 to 10 cm). Male and females are visually similar, but males have a brighter, more iridescent blue coloring on their hindwings compared to the females. Both sexes have light marginal and submarginal spots on both forewings and hindwings on the dorsal surface. The ventral hindwings have

A male pipevine swallowtail feeding on Ironweed.

A female pipevine swallowtail in a Florida garden.

ABOVE: Dutchman's pipevine is the primary source of food for pipevine swallowtail larvae. RIGHT: A pipevine swallowtail chrysalis held by two thin threads.

blue iridescence and a row of seven bright-orange submarginal spots. There is also a row of white spots on the lateral part of the abdomen. Males have striking iridescent blue on hindwings, while females have these same iridescent blue hindwings, but duller than the males. Additionally, the white spots on the dorsal forewings and hindwings are larger and more prominent on the females.

Dimorphism: Sexual yes, seasonal yes, albeit more pronounced as a regional dimorphism, with eastern forms being larger, less hairy, and possessing longer thoracic filaments than their western counterparts

Generations: 2 to 3, depending on region

Lifespan: Adult butterflies live for about a month.

Eggs: The eggs are reddish-orange. They are also covered in a hard, nutritious secretion laid down in vertical bands, with large droplets in the bands. They are usually laid in clusters on stems and leaves of young, tender growing shoot tips. This stage typically lasts between 4 and 10 days.

Larvae: Larvae can reach about 2 inches (5 cm) in length. They start off being orangish-brown, with short orange tubercles and setae, but become glossy, dark brown or black, with subdorsal and lateral rows of bright orange and red tubercles. This stage lasts around 3 to 4 weeks.

Number of instars: 5

Chrysalis: Chrysalids can be green or brown, and the sides of the body are widened into lateral flanges. These flanges can be bluish-purple. Spring and summer broods form green chrysalids attached to green leaves and stems, whereas overwintering chrysalids are brown and attach to non-deciduous materials, such as bark or stone. This stage lasts ten to 20 days (not including overwintering time).

Range: Eastern Canada; south to Florida, west to Nebraska through Texas into Arizona and California.

Larval host plants: Dutchman's pipevine, *Aristolochia* spp.

Nectar sources: Butterfly bush, coneflowers, ironweed, milkweed, phlox, thistle, zinnias

Migration or overwintering: Overwinters as a chrysalis.

Fun fact: These butterflies may not emerge as an adult (eclose) from their overwintering chrysalis the following spring; some may take up to three or four years to eclose!

Spicebush Swallowtail

Papilio troilus

Description: The population trend of the spicebush swallowtail is considered generally stable. Their preferred habitats are forest margins, gardens, meadows, parks, pastures, pine barrens, roadsides, deciduous woodlands, and wooded swamps. There are at least three generations in the deep south and two generations in the north, with flights peaking between late spring and early fall. Their flight pattern is described as strong and agile, characterized by a combination of rapid wingbeats and glides, with

A female spicebush swallowtail nectaring on butterfly weed.

A male spicebush swallowtail nectaring on fire pink.

A spicebush butterfly caterpillar with its distinctive eyespots.

A spicebush butterfly chrysalis hanging from a spicebush stem.

flights at a low level close to the ground. Adult butterflies are 3½ to 4¾ inches (9 to 12 cm). The upper surface of the forewings is black with a narrow marginal row and a broader submarginal row of light yellowish spots. The upper surfaces of the hindwings also feature these rows of spots, but they are green in color. The undersides of the hindwings have marginal pale green spots and marginal and post-median rows of bright orange spots, separated by black and blue patches. In females, the median area of the hindwings is dusted with blue; male hindwings are blue-green, which can vary greatly. Males exhibit puddling behavior.

Dimorphism: Sexual yes, seasonal no

Generations: 2 to 3, depending on region

Lifespan: Adult butterflies live for one to two weeks.

Eggs: The eggs are spherical and greenish white or transparent white. Larvae are visible shortly before hatching. Eggs are laid singly on the undersides of the new host plant leaves. This stage lasts around ten days.

Larvae: Initially, young larvae resemble bird droppings, providing camouflage that helps to protect them from predators. As the caterpillars mature, they transform into bright green larvae with large, snake-like eyespots on their thorax. This stage lasts around three to four weeks.

Number of instars: 5

Chrysalis: Pupae have two anterior horns and may be either green or brown. Twenty-four hours before eclosing, the adult butterfly becomes visible through the transparent pupal cuticle. Overwintering pupae are brown. This stage lasts around 10 to 20 days (not including overwintering time).

Range: Eastern North America to the Rockies

Larval host plants: Spicebush, sassafras, bays

Nectar sources: Agastache, buttonbush, coneflowers, honeysuckle, ironweeds, Joe-Pye weed, lantana

Migration or overwintering: Non-migratory; overwinters as a chrysalid.

Fun fact: Larval changes as they mature are an example of mimicry. First, they resemble bird droppings, and later, they resemble snakes or frogs, both of which serve as effective defense mechanisms against predation. To me, they look like a business opportunity for the design of a pool toy!

Western Tiger Swallowtail

Papilio rutulus

Description: The population trend of the western tiger swallowtail is generally considered stable. Their preferred habitats include parks, roadsides, riparian areas, woodlands near rivers and streams, wooded suburbs, and urban areas. At higher elevations, they have one main brood and flight from June to July, but can have one to three broods and flights from late February to October in lower elevations, such as in Washington. Their flight pattern is known as graceful and gliding, with minimal flapping. Male western tiger swallowtails, like the eastern tiger swallowtails, are yellow with dark tiger stripes, with limited blue coloring. Females have two forms: one yellow, like the male, or a dark form, black with shadows of dark stripes. Both female forms have blue chevrons and an iridescent blue wash over parts of

A female western tiger swallowtail (yellow form) nectaring on non-native ivy geranium.

A male western tiger swallowtail.

A female western tiger swallowtail (black form) nectaring on non-native Plumbago auriculata.

A western tiger swallowtail caterpillar.

A western tiger swallowtail chrysalis looks similar to an eastern tiger swallowtail chrysalis.

the interior hindwing. Their wingspan ranges from 2¾ to 4 inches (7 to 10 cm). The primary difference between the western and eastern tiger swallowtail is geographic location, with the western tiger swallowtail found in the Rocky Mountains and west. The black form female tiger swallowtail protects itself by mimicking the pipevine swallowtail, which is toxic to many predators. Predators avoid both.

Dimorphism: Sexual no, seasonal yes, with spring forms being smaller and paler than their summer counterparts

Generations: 1 to 3, depending on region

Lifespan: Adults live between 6 and 14 days.

Eggs: Dark green, glossy, and spherical. They are laid singly on the underside of host plant leaves. This stage typically lasts between 4 and 10 days.

Larvae: Young larvae resemble bird droppings, with a mottled appearance of white, tan, and brown. Later instar larvae become smooth with green coloring and false eyes. Their eyespots are yellow with black and blue markings. Before pupating, they turn brown, and a prominent orange with a black pupil eyespot replaces the eyespots on the third segment. This stage lasts between three and four weeks.

Number of instars: 5

Chrysalis: Pupae are brown and have a girdle, fastened head up on the side or underside of logs, branches, fences, or house siding. This stage lasts 10 to 20 days (excluding overwintering time).

Range: Rockies and west from Washington to California

Larval host plants: Note some differences in host plants between Eastern and Western swallowtail host plants, alders, aspens, ashes, cottonwoods, wild cherry, and willows

Nectar sources: Agapanthus, blazing star, coneflowers, ironweeds, Joe-Pye weed, oregano, and zinnias.

Migration or overwintering: Non-migratory; instead, they'll move to other areas when resources are scarce. These butterflies overwinter as chrysalides.

Fun fact: One female may lay up to one hundred eggs at a time.

Zebra Swallowtail

Eurytides marcellus

Description: The population of the zebra swallowtail is generally declining; between 2000 and 2020, the population experienced a cumulative decrease of approximately 67%. Their preferred habitats include moist areas, such as low-lying woodlands, and especially near bodies of water, including lakes, marshes, and rivers, where pawpaws are commonly found. They have two broods in the north, from April to August. In the south, there can be up to four broods between March and December. They tend to fly close to the ground using shallow wingbeats, and their flight is often described as bat-like and erratic. Their wingspan ranges from 2½ to 4 inches (6 to 10 cm). It has long, triangular wings with swordlike tails extending from its hindwings. They range from white to greenish white, with black longitudinal stripes. A red stripe runs along the middle of the ventral hindwing. The summer forms are larger

A zebra swallowtail nectaring on a butterfly bush. Males and females are visually similar to each other.

A zebra swallowtail caterpillar.

than their spring forms, with light blue-green wings, broader black stripes, and longer, black tails with white edges. Male and female zebra swallowtail butterflies are visually similar. Small groups of patrolling males often form near mud puddles or moist streambanks—a behavior known as puddling.

Dimorphism: Sexual no, seasonal yes, characterized by a smaller spring form and shorter, black tails with white tips

Generations: 2 to 3, depending on region

Lifespan: Adult butterflies can live up to six months.

Eggs: Laid singly on the underside of pawpaw leaves. They are spherical in shape and translucent green when laid but become peachy and mottled as they age. This stage lasts 4 to 10 days.

Larvae: Caterpillars are hairless. There are several larval forms: initially black with lighter transverse bands. Then transitioning to green with yellow and black bands. Some larvae may exhibit a darker form with orange and white bands. They have a humped appearance, with a yellow, forked, foul-smelling osmeterium that deters predators.

Number of instars: 5

Chrysalis: The pupa is attached to a stem or leaf by the tail and by a girdle of silk around the thorax, hanging head upwards in this position. It can range from brown to green in color. It also has three small horn-like projections. This stage lasts for about 10 to 20 days (not including overwintering time).

Range: East coast, south to Florida and the Gulf of Mexico.

Larval host plants: Pawpaw trees (*Asimina trilobal*)

Nectar sources: Boneset, ironweeds, Joe-Pye weed, milkweeds, tickseed sunflower

Migration or overwintering: Non-migratory; overwinters as a chrysalis on its host plant

Fun fact: The caterpillar exclusively feeds on the leaves of the pawpaw tree. The leaves contain a toxin that the caterpillar absorbs, making it distasteful to predators.

Gossamer-Wingeds (Coppers, Blues, and Hairstreaks)

Family: Lycaenidae; Subfamilies: Lycaenidae (Coppers), Polyommatinae (Blues), Theclinae (Hairstreaks)

Description: The Lycaenidae family population trend is declining. A diverse group of butterflies, Lycaenidae are characterized by their small size, delicate wings, and bright colors. "Gossamer" may not be a term often used in everyday conversations, unless you're talking about butterflies. Gossamer describes a fabric characterized by being sheer, soft, and thin, similar to gauze. The wing delicacy of the Lycaenidae butterflies is well-suited to the word gossamer.

As the common name suggests, Coppers exhibit a tinge of copper coloring in their wings, along with orange-red to brown wings and dark markings. Coppers are widespread throughout the regions north of Mexico, with 15 known species. The approximate number of species north of Mexico is upwards of 150.

The population of the subfamily Polyommatinae (blues) is declining. Blues are characterized by their wings' blue coloration, particularly in males, which reflects blue light due to the nanostructure of their scales. Females often have brown wings with blue dusting and orange spots. Blues are widespread north of Mexico with upwards of 135 known species.

Gossamer-winged butterflies have a unique relationship with ants, known as myrmecophily, which translates to "ant love." Their symbiotic relationship is such that the ants protect these butterfly larvae in exchange for a sugary reward that the caterpillars secrete.

An example of myrmecophily, the symbiotic relationship between some ants and butterfly larvae.

A gray hairstreak butterfly.

Purplish Copper

Lycaena helloides

Description: The population trend of the purplish copper is stable. Its wingspan ranges from 1 to 1½ inches (3 to 4 cm). Their preferred habitats are marshes, meadows, open fields, roadsides, and stream edges, where they can find their host plants. Purplish coppers may also be found in montane and alpine areas up to 10,000 feet.

Dimorphism: Sexual yes, seasonal no

Generations: 2 or 3

Lifespan: Adults live between 7 and 14 days.

Eggs: Purplish coppers lay greenish-white and ribbed eggs singly and haphazardly at the base of the host plant, on host plant leaves, and complex flower heads. As the eggs mature, they turn completely white. The egg stage ranges from 5 to 6 days.

Larvae: Solitary, red to light green or yellow larvae, with a slug-like appearance, and covered with short hairs. The larval stage ranges from 17 to 24 days.

Number of instars: 4

Chrysalis: Light brown with many dark colored dots. Pupation occurs under shelter such as stones, logs, or boards. The chrysalis stage lasts about 7 days.

Range: California, most common in the far west; seen in the northwest and the Great Lakes area

Larval host plants: Buckwheat, cinquefoils, curly dock, knotweeds, sheep sorrel

Nectar sources: Asters, buttercups, clovers, knotweeds, pearly everlastings, and many other composites

Migration or overwinter: Non-migratory; overwinters as eggs.

Fun fact: The common name arises from the purplish sheen of a recently emerged male butterfly.

A purplish copper butterfly nectaring on yarrow.

Marine Blue

Leptotes marina

Description: The population trend is considered generally stable. The marine blue's wingspan is ⅞ to 1⅛ inches (2 to 3 cm). Their preferred habitat includes areas that are subtropical and southwestern, as well as open areas such as mesquite scrub, alfalfa fields, deserts, gardens, grasslands, old fields, pastures, and waste areas.

Dimorphism: Sexual yes, seasonal no

Generations: Multiple

Lifespan: 5 to 10 days

Eggs: Initially green, maturing to white, eggs are laid singly on the host plant's flower buds. The egg stage ranges from 3 to 6 days.

Larvae: Green, brown, or reddish, ribbed bodies, with a slug-like appearance. Young larvae are tiny and camouflage themselves to resemble a leaf. Marine Blues feed on flower buds, developing seeds, rarely on petals, and not on host plant leaves. The larval stage ranges from 2 to 3 weeks.

Number of instars: 5

Chrysalis: Mottled brown with a slug-like appearance. Marine Blue pupate in soil or leaf litter. The chrysalis stage ranges from 7 to 10 days.

Range: Central Pacific coast, through Texas and north into the midwest

Larval host plants: Legumes such as alfalfa, deerweed, false indigo, milkvetch, mesquites, plumbago, and wisteria

Nectar sources: Alfalfa, aster, blazing star, coneflower, chives, clover, coreopsis, dandelion, goldenrod, hyssop, lantana, lavender, milkweed, mints, sunflower, oregano

Migration or overwintering: Marine blues migrate northward and up in elevation in warmer months and return south as temperatures drop. They live year-round in southern climates.

Fun fact: These butterflies are extremely adaptable, having been one of the few native North American butterflies that has made a switch to a new larval host plant introduced from South Africa and to a nectar source and an ant from South America, none of which are closely related to its native resources.

A marine blue nectaring on Cape Marguerite.

Gray Hairstreak

Strymon melinus

Description: Overall, the population trend for hairstreaks is declining. Characterized by their small size, often brown or iridescent blue, with the presence of hindwings, hairstreaks are widespread throughout regions north of Mexico, with upwards of 90 species. The adult wingspan ranges from ⅞ to 1⅜ inches (2 to 3.5 cm). Their preferred areas include agricultural areas, gardens, Grasslands, montane meadows, open weedy regions, river basins, and sagebrush steppe.

Dimorphism: Sexual yes, seasonal yes

Generations: 3 or more

Lifespan: 3 to 4 weeks

Eggs: Green eggs with a delicate net-like appearance are laid singly on host plant inflorescences, flower buds, fruits, small leaves near flowers, and seeds. The egg stage lasts about 6 days.

Larvae: Straw, purplish-pink, reddish-brown, or green in color with various paler marks, and a yellowish-brown head. The larval stage lasts about 20 days.

Number of instars: 4

Chrysalis: Typically brownish with darker spotting

Range: North America

Larval host plants: Beans, bush clover, buckwheat, clovers, hops, mints

Nectar sources: California lilacs, goldenrods, Joe-Pye weed, oregano, veronicas

Migration or overwinter: Non-migratory; overwinters as a chrysalid.

Fun fact: Gray hairstreak butterflies have false heads, perching with their head downward and their two sets of tails and eyespots pointed upward, moving in a sawing motion to attract attention to the rear wing instead of their real head.

A gray hairstreak resting on a leaf in California.

Skippers

Family: Hesperiidae;
Subfamilies: Hesperinae, Pyrginae

Description: Skipper populations are declining, as they rely on prairie ecosystems, and many prairies have been converted to agricultural land, fragmenting the prairie landscape. A recent study showed a 22% drop in skipper populations between 2000 and 2020. Skipper butterflies belong to the family Hesperiidae, with two Subfamilies: Hesperinae, known as grass skippers, and Pyrginae, known as spread-winged skippers. The grass skippers are not included in this book, since most lay their eggs on grasses and sedges. I have focused on native forbs, broad-leaved herbaceous plants. Pyrginae, spread-wing skippers, have around 100 species north of Mexico.

It's interesting to note that while skippers are butterflies, they aren't often immediately recognized as such. There are several reasons for this, including their antennae, body shape, flight pattern, and wing posture. Unlike the club-shaped antennae of most butterflies, skippers' antennae are hooked-tipped. Skippers' bodies are chunky and are often mistaken for moths. When resting, other butterflies typically hold their wings vertically above their backs; skippers, however, vary the position of their wings when at rest, sometimes holding their wings with their forewings held at a different angle to the hindwings, or in a partially open position. Plus, as their common name suggests, skippers' flight is characterized by darting, rapid, or erratic patterns.

California lilac provides a paradise for many important pollinators.

Common Checkered Skipper

Burnsius communis

Description: The population of common checkered skippers is relatively stable. Their wingspan is 1 to 1½ inches wide (3 to 4 cm). Their preferred habitats include gardens, highway shoulders, landfills, montane forest openings, and areas above alpine tree lines, pastures, prairies, urban parks, wet and dry meadows, and woodlands.

Dimorphism: Sexual yes, seasonal no

Generations: 2 in northern regions; multiple, overlapping in the southern areas.

Lifespan: 2 to 4 weeks

Eggs: Whitish, spherical-shaped with many ridges. Eggs are laid singly, mostly on leaf buds, both surfaces of leaves, and mostly near leaf margins. The egg stage ranges from 3 to 5 days.

Larvae: Pale yellowish green color with a darker green stripe running the length of the upper body and two white stripes along each side. Their body is covered in fine, white hairs and tiny tubercles, with black heads densely covered in white hair. Their collar is light brown at the front, and black at the back with a short white line in the middle. The first two pairs of their legs are darker.

Number of instars: 5

Chrysalis: Light brown near the head and fades into light green at the thorax area. The abdominal area is yellowish. There are black dots and dashes that form bands on the upper surface, and the wing cases are a greenish hue. They will pupate under the webbing of silk within a nest, on an inert surface, away from the host plant, or may even pupate in soil. The chrysalis stage ranges between 11 to 12 days.

Range: Canada through Central America

Larval host plants: In the mallow family, including various native hibiscus species, *Hibiscus* spp., and non-native weeds like the low-growing "cheeses" and hollyhocks, *Alcea rosea*. While hollyhocks are non-native, I grow them because they are a common host plant for the checkered skipper butterfly.

Nectar sources: Mostly from white-flowering composites such as asters, fleabane, shepherd's needles, and also red clover.

Migration or overwintering: Non-migratory. Overwinters as L4 and L5 instars.

Fun fact: These butterflies are mostly solitary, only aggregating in large numbers to mate.

A common checkered skipper butterfly.

Brush-Footeds (Emperors, Monarchs, Fritillaries, Longwings, Satyrs)

Family: Nymphalidae; Subfamilies: Apaturinae, Danainae, Heliconiinae, Nymphalinae, Satyrinae, plus Seven Others

Description: The population trends of the Nymphalidae butterfly family are declining, with varying degrees of decline among different species. The family Nymphalidae is the largest butterfly family, including monarchs, viceroys, and fritillaries. Monarchs receive a great deal of attention, and rightfully so. Today, the monarch butterfly is likely the best known of the brush-footeds.

Learning about the decline of the Monarch butterfly has opened the minds and hearts to other butterfly declines. It took the tragic decline of the Monarch butterfly population to breathe new life into conservation. As a gardener, you may not think of yourself as a conservationist, but you are or can be. I am a conservationist through native plant gardening.

Eliminating the use of pesticides is the first step, followed by adding butterfly host plants, which is paramount not just for the Brush-footed, but for all butterfly families.

Brush-footed butterflies are characterized by reduced forelegs, typically held against their body and not used for walking. Their modified forelegs enable them to clean and groom themselves, giving them a brush-like appearance. With these two forelegs held closely, it gives the butterfly the appearance of only having four legs, hence their other common name, the four-footed butterflies.

The butterflies featured include border patch, comma, fritillaries, pearl crescent, question mark, and, yes, the monarch butterfly. I have a particular fondness for the fritillaries. This stems from their host plant, the common violet, which grass lovers are trying to eliminate from grass. I hope my discussions will give the lowly violet new appreciation.

The painted lady is a widespread species, found on all but two of the world's continents.

Monarch

Danaus plexippus

Description: The population trend is declining. The western monarchs have experienced a 95% decline since the 1980s. The eastern populations have seen an 80% decline since the 1990s. There was a recent rise from the steady eastern decline, to make us hopeful, but only time will tell if it will continue that trend. The wingspan ranges from 3⅜ to 4⅞ inches (8.6 to 12 cm), making them some of the largest butterfly species in their habitats. Monarch butterflies prefer open areas with their host plants, milkweeds (*Asclepias* spp.), which are found in gardens, grasslands, meadows, prairies, and on roadsides.

Dimorphism: Sexual yes, seasonal no

Generations: 4 or 5

Lifespan: 2 to 6 weeks during the summer breeding season. The last generation of the year, which enters diapause and migrates for the winter, can live for 6 to 9 months.

A female monarch nectaring on New England aster.

A monarch larva in the classic J-shaped stage before forming the chrysalis.

The smooth, jade-green monarch chrysalis.

Eggs: Creamy white or yellow eggs, laid singly under the leaves of milkweed plants, oval and slightly pointed, with vertical ridges.

Larvae: Initially, pale green or grayish-white larvae, shiny and translucent with black heads. Their characteristic black, yellow, and white stripes begin to form once they start feeding.

Number of instars: 5

Chrysalis: a jade green, vase-shaped chrysalis with gold accents and a smooth, hard shell, reminiscent of an Egyptian Sarcophagus. Very cool looking!

Range: Canada south through all of the United States, Central America, and most of South America

Larval host plants: Milkweed plants (*Asclepias* spp.)

Favored nectar plants: Blazing stars, dogbane, goldenrods, ironweed, lilac, red clover, lantana, sunflowers, thistles

Migration or overwintering: Most eastern Monarchs undertake a long migration to Mexico and overwinter there as adults, whereas most western Monarchs undertake a shorter migration, staying within the western region and also overwintering there as adults.

Fun fact: Most milkweeds contain cardiac glycosides, which are stored in the bodies of both the caterpillar and the adult. These poisons are distasteful and emetic to birds and other vertebrate predators.

One of many clusters of hundreds of thousands of monarch butterflies overwintering on a Mexican oyamel fir tree.

The Wonders of Monarch Butterfly Migration

The US has two Monarch migrations—the eastern, and the western.

The Eastern Migration

The eastern migration involves Monarch butterflies that have bred east of the Rocky Mountains and their subsequent migration south to Mexico for the winter months. Monarchs overwinter in the forest of oyamel fir, *Abies religiosa*, in central Mexico.

These millions of non-breeding Monarch butterflies gather in the Sierra Madre mountains, including the Sierra Madre Oriental and the Sierra Gorda ranges. The oyamel fir forest grows on south-facing slopes in these mountains at 2 miles above sea level. A key overwintering area is the Monarch Butterfly Biosphere Reserve, located in Michoacán and the State of Mexico. These fir forests offer a microclimate with temperatures above freezing and shelter from minimal predator attacks. Monarch butterflies conserve energy and survive the winter in these forests.

The overwintering site is a period of reduced activity and metabolism, effectively a state of hibernation. During diapause, Monarchs suspend their reproductive processes and focus on accumulating fat reserves for the return journey north in the spring.

I was fortunate enough to travel to Mexico in February 2020 and spend four days at Cerro Pelon Butterfly B&B, which I reached via a two-and-a-half-hour bus ride from Mexico City. While in Cerro Pelon, a mule ride took us farther up the mountain to spend a quiet respite and see and hear millions of Monarch butterflies gathering on the oyamel fir trees. It was an unforgettable experience. If you ever get an opportunity like this, it mustn't be missed.

During the spring migration, from March through May, Monarch butterflies begin their long journey north from Mexico through Texas. They generally follow a path through the southern US and move north into central latitudes, reaching as far as southern Canada. They are looking to lay eggs on their only host plant, milkweed, Asclepias spp. Typically, Texas produces the first generation of Monarchs because it's where milkweed plants are found. Several generations will continue as the Monarch butterfly travels north, laying eggs and living for only a few weeks, passing on the journey to the next generation.

When a Monarch butterfly migrates south to Mexico in the fall, there are four to five generations that are required to make the journey. Let's give that further thought—the Monarch butterfly that leaves Mexico in the spring for its journey north is the great-, great-, great-, or more grand butterfly to the one that returns south again in the fall. It's a mystery how this is accomplished, especially given that they often return even to the same tree.

Millions of butterflies from the central and eastern Canadian provinces and the eastern and midwestern US migrate to Mexico. Their flight pattern is shaped like a funnel as they come together and pass over the state of Texas on their way farther south.

Each generation, except the last, lives for only a few weeks, passing on its genetics to the next. The last generation, also known as the super generation, migrates south and lives much longer, sometimes up to eight months, because they enter diapause, a state of hormonal dormancy, which allows them to survive the winter.

These overwintering Monarchs are the only Monarchs left that can produce a new generation east of the Rockies. They cannot lay their eggs if they return north too early, before the milkweed is present in the spring.

An interesting note: It wasn't until 1975 that a scientific team led by Dr. Fred Urquhart, with help from his wife, Norah, finally tracked down the Monarch butterflies' wintering sites in Mexico. Until then, the winter hideouts had been a secret known only to local villagers.

The Western Migration

The western Monarch migration isn't quite as intriguing—it involves traveling to coastal California for the winter. These Monarchs overwinter in clusters on eucalyptus (*Eucalyptus* spp.), Monterey cypress (*Cupressus macrocarpa*), and other hosts, then disperse in the spring.

Sadly, these overwintering sites have suffered significant diminishment due to the clearing of trees for shopping malls, highways, and new housing developments. The remaining sites offer a specific microclimate that enables Monarchs to conserve energy and await the spring breeding season.

In the spring, western Monarchs disperse from their overwintering sites along the California coast to various locations within the western US in search of milkweed plants. They eventually disperse throughout California, Oregon, Washington, and Idaho. Like the eastern Monarchs, the western Monarchs will return to their overwintering site after three or four generations, with the last generation going into diapause and living the longest.

More active monarchs fill the air at their Mexican overwintering spot.

Great Spangled Fritillary

Speyeria cybele

Description: The population trend is generally declining. The wingspan ranges between 2½ and 4 inches (6 and 10 cm), making them some of the largest species in their habitats. They prefer open, moist habitats.

Dimorphism: Sexual yes, seasonal no

Generations: 1

Lifespan: 30 to 45 days

Eggs: Faint grayish-white eggs are laid singly on the leaves of host plants in late summer. The egg stage ranges from 2 to 3 weeks.

Larvae: Jet-black body with spine-like structures, each spine tipped with an orange spot. The larval stage ranges from 2 to 4 weeks.

Number of instars: 6

Chrysalis: Glossy chestnut black or brown with black and yellow abdominal spines. The chrysalis stage ranges from 2 to 3 weeks.

Range: Most of the US, except the deep south and extreme southwest; north into eastern Canada

Larval host plants: Violets

Nectar sources: Bee balm, coneflowers, dogbane, ironweed, Joe-Pye weed, milkweeds, mountain laurel, verbena, red clover.

Migration or overwintering: Non-migratory. Overwinters as an L1 instar.

Fun fact: Larvae enter a dormant state and don't feed or move until the spring when their sole host plant—violets—is available.

A great spangled fritillary larva feeding on violet.

A great spangled fritillary nectaring on dogbane.

Painted Lady

Vanessa cardui

Description: Some studies suggest that the population is declining, but the painted lady is considered to be large and widespread, with an increase in both abundance and distribution. Wingspan 2 to 2⅞ inches (5 to 7 cm). Their preferred habitats include a wide range of sunny, open areas such as fields, gardens, grasslands, meadows, urban areas, and woodlands.

Dimorphism: Sexual yes, slight; seasonal yes

Generations: 5

Lifespan: 2 to 3 weeks

Eggs: Pale green eggs are laid singly on the leaves of many different host plants. Females lay eggs on plants with flowers, so adults are nectar ready for adults to

A painted lady nectaring on lesser knapweed.

A painted lady chrysalis.

feed on, despite the high mortality of the larvae due to volatile chemicals released from host plants. This stage lasts about 3 to 5 days.

Larvae: Grayish brown or purple-black, spiny larvae with yellow side stripes. The larval stage ranges from 5 to 10 days.

Number of instars: 5

Chrysalis: Beige with a hint of lavender, typically smooth and cylindrical. The chrysalis stage ranges from 7 to 10 days.

Range: North America

Larval host plants: Asters and others in the daisy family; thistle

Nectar sources: Asters, vervain, butterfly bush, chaste tree, Mexican sunflower, zinnias

Migration or overwintering: Considered long-distance northern migrants, yet they do not follow seasonal changes and are more sporadic. It takes about six generations for the painted lady's round-trip journey from Mexico to Canada and back.

Fun fact: They are the most widespread butterfly species in the world, found on every continent except Australia and Antarctica. Also, they can fly at speeds up to 30 mph!

CHAPTER 3

Hummingbirds

Hummingbirds are spiritual to many, including me. They symbolize joy, happiness, swiftness, and resilience. They remind me to live in the moment, something that we struggle to do. With so many distractions around us, quick visits from hummingbirds teach us to sit and admire the pollinators.

Great joy overcomes me when I see the first spring hummingbird's arrival. Where I'm located, in North Carolina, we only host the ruby-throated hummingbird, *Archilochus colubris*, but it's enough for me. Yes, I hope to see each of the species that nest and breed throughout the United States. It would be best if I started this new journey in northern California, home to several hummingbird species, such as Anna's hummingbird, *Calypte anna*, and Allen's hummingbird, *Selasphorus sasinas*, which are year-round residents. The calliope, *Selasphorus callioperufous*, and the black-chinned hummingbird,

A black-chinned hummingbird feeding on a thistle.

Two Anna's hummingbirds waiting to be fed.

Selasphorus calliope, can also be seen during their breeding or migratory periods in northern California.

I often forget hummingbirds are, in fact, birds. They are so unique in the world of birds that it is no wonder that when the first Europeans arrived in the New World and saw the ruby-throated hummingbird, they were unsure of what they were. That's because hummingbirds didn't exist in Europe. Early European explorers wondered if the migrating hummingbird was a cross between a bird and an insect, and they referred to them as "flybirds."

Mating

Hummingbirds don't mate for life. The male will begin to entice a female in his territory by performing a courtship display, demonstrating he is the best male for the female. If she liked his display, she will mate with him. If not, she moves on to another territory. She doesn't have to go far; a male's territory is about ¼ acre.

The female hummingbird is the sole nest builder and caregiver for her brood, incubating the eggs and feeding her chicks. Their broods are fed a mixture of regurgitated nectar (providing carbohydrates) and small insects (providing protein) for quick development. She rocks!

Nesting

Sadly, I've never seen a hummingbird's nest in nature, and it's not for the lack of trying. The east coast of America, where I live, is home to the ruby-throated hummingbird, which breeds and nests during the summer months. Yet, their nests have eluded me, as they are super small and built at heights ranging from 10 to 40 feet (3 to 10 meters), so they aren't easily spotted. The average size of a hummingbird's nest is about the size of a half-dollar coin. Nests are built along a forked branch, about the size of a pencil.

Don't be so quick to remove spiderwebs! Hummingbirds use spiderwebs to help bind their nests together. For the rest of the structure, hummers use lichen, moss, and even bits of plastic. Keeping spider webs up will also attract insects, which will be caught in the spider's web—food for the hummingbirds.

Feeding Hummingbirds in Your Garden

A hummingbird garden requires more than pretty, tubular-shaped, nectar-rich flowers. Seeing hummingbirds visit our selected flowers is delightful, but did you know that, according to naturalist and author Doug Tallamy, upwards of 80% of a hummingbird's diet consists of soft-bodied insects? This is another reason why it is essential not to use pesticides. Hummingbirds even eat mosquitoes!

Hummingbirds favor locations within their range that present plentiful natural nectar sources and well-placed feeders. We can help them by providing both! In fact, many researchers attribute the hummingbird's population stabilization to gardeners' increased offering of well-maintained sugar water feeders

Hummingbirds hover midair to sip nectar from flowers and feeders, flapping their wings between 720 to 5,400 wing beats per minute. The ruby-throated hummingbird beats its wings about 53 times a second. Think about that! Hummingbirds' dense muscles enable such speed, with 25% to 30% of a bird's weight in its pectoral muscles. Their wings move in a figure-8 pattern, allowing them to maneuver with ease, propelling them forward and upside down. And they are the only birds that can fly backward.

Many think of a hummingbird's tongue as straw-like; instead, the tongue is flat and split at the tip, bifurcated like a forked tongue. During flight, a hummingbird compresses its tongue, building up

Native coral honeysuckle, *Lonicera sempervirens*.

LEFT: A juvenile male ruby-throated with his tongue out. BELOW: A female hummingbird feeding insects to her chicks.

potential energy. When finding nectar, the tongue's grooves open, creating a vacuum that pulls in the nectar. The tongue then retracts, squeezing the nectar from the grooves into the bird's throat.

Protein

Let hummingbirds be your pest control: hummingbirds will feed on your pesky soft-bodied insects—gnats, aphids, fruit flies, mosquitoes, and spiders. It's a win-win! Hummingbirds also feed on wasps, larvae, and insect eggs. To attract insects, leave spider cobwebs in place (with insects still attached) or offer mashed bananas, oranges, or chunks of watermelon. They will draw insects that hummingbirds will feed on.

Nectar

In general, hummingbirds prefer trumpet-shaped flowers to feed on while in flight. And hummingbirds will feed from feeders filled with sugar water that matches the sweetness level of floral delights. It's a myth that keeping feeders up in the fall or winter will prevent hummingbirds from migrating. However, it may help a straggler who is late to migrate or off course, so I keep my nectar water maintained until the first frost.

How to Make Hummingbird Nectar

Having a hummingbird feeder hung where you can enjoy watching the hummingbirds feed can be an enriching experience. While I have dozens of trumpet-shaped flowers for hummers to feed upon, hanging dedicated feeders off my back porch lets me view them up close and personal. Hosting a hummingbird feeder also comes with responsibilities.

Hummingbird feeders are different from seed or suet feeders, where you fill and refill them once the seed is spent. For a hummingbird feeder, plan on supplying the sugar water often, even daily, and never, ever use honey as a sugar source—honey can promote dangerous fungal growth.

The viability of sugar water is temperature-dependent. You can't go wrong emptying and refilling the feeder daily in the summer. At 90°F, a sugar water feeder will ferment in a day, but worse, the mixture will mold, and fungus will begin to sprout. The temperature in the 60s can go a couple of days or up to a week before refilling.

By drinking fermented water, a hummingbird could become sick or even die. Fermented sugar water can cause their tongues to swell, prohibiting feeding. And just like us, but faster, alcohol can fatally enlarge their tiny livers.

What about those pretty red-dyed mixes? Undoubtedly, the extra punch of red will help attract hummingbirds, but it isn't necessary, and can be harmful. Most feeders have enough red to attract birds. The Cornell Lab of Ornithology strongly recommends against using red dye in feeders.

Before we get into making our hummingbird sugar water, here's an interesting hummingbird fact: Hummingbirds have fantastic memories. Their brains account for 4.2% of their body weight, whereas human brains account for only 2%. (So, where exactly did I put my keys?!) Their memories are remarkable, especially when it comes to food.

A hummingbird remembers every flower visit, including the ones on its migration route. It knows how long it has been since it last visited a particular bloom and doesn't revisit until the flower has had time to produce more nectar.

Remember, make fresh sugar water and change out your hummingbirds' food supply daily.

A hummingbird at a nectar feeder.

Hummingbird Nectar Recipe

¼ cup sugar
1 cup boiling water

1. In a saucepan, dissolve the sugar in the hot water, then allow the mixture to cool.

2. Fill the feeder with the sugar water, then hang the feeder outside.

Anna's Hummingbird

Calypte anna

Description: The Anna's hummingbird population has shown an increase since the 1970s, primarily due to the species' ability to adapt to human habitats, including the widespread use of sugar water feeders and the addition of trumpet-shaped flowering plants in gardens. Interestingly, the population increase has also been attributed to the rise in non-native trumpet-shaped flowers. Anna's hummingbirds are considered stocky for a hummingbird, with a length ranging from 4 to 4¼ inches (10 to 11 cm) and a wingspan of 4¾ inches (12 cm). Their preferred habitats include open woodlands, chaparral, coastal scrub, and oak savannas. The species is named after Italian noblewoman Anna Masséna, duchess of Rivoli, by French naturalist René-Primevère Lesson in 1829. The duchess likely never saw Anna's hummingbird in the wild. As a non-migratory bird, Anna's have a longer lifespan than other hummingbirds. The male is characterized by its bright, iridescent rose-red gorget, throat, and crown. The iridescent colors on the head

A male Anna's at a nectar feeder.

A female Anna's on a creosote brush.

and crown are structural, meaning they are created by the way light reflects off the feather structure, rather than being pigment. As such, depending on the light and angle of observation, the gorget and crown can appear dark or even black. Anna's male bodies are generally a glossy, dark green above and gray-green below. Females are similar in size to the males but lack the male's bright pink gorget, with a duller green and gray coloration of the throat, breast, and belly.

Dimorphism: Sexual yes, seasonal no

Lifespan: Male and female: 8½ years

Breeding range: Along the Pacific coast of North America, from British Columbia south to northern Baja California, Mexico, and inland to parts of Arizona, Nevada, and Utah.

Nesting: 4 to 25 feet (1 to 7.6 meters) above ground

Eggs: 2

Generations: 2 or 3

Migration or overwintering: Anna's Hummingbirds are year-round residents. Some individuals may migrate short distances in response to changes in elevation and variations in food availability.

Nectar sources: Agapanthus, bee balm, columbine, coral honeysuckle, crocosmia, eucalyptus, fuchsia-flowering gooseberry, lantana, milkweed, monkey flowers, penstemon, phlox, red gooseberry, red-hot poker, scarlet sage, tree tobacco, trumpet vine

Fun fact: I once saw an Anna's Hummingbird in the Outer Banks of North Carolina. Most definitely, it must have caught the jet stream. The breeding range for the Anna's hummingbird was originally exclusive to northern Baja California and southern California; however, this bird's range has expanded thanks to the planting of exotic flowering trees.

Black-Chinned Hummingbird

Archilochus alexandri

Description: The population trend is good news—from 1970 to 2019, the population of the black-chinned hummingbird increased by 52%. The rise in population is likely due to the popularity of backyard hummingbird feeders. The black-chinned hummingbird is one of the most adaptable hummingbirds, often found in urban areas, recently disturbed habitats, and pristine natural areas. The males have a distinctive appearance, characterized by a black head and chin, a glossy purple throat patch or gorget, and a white underside. Females lack the black chin and are slightly larger than the males, with a duller, greenish-gray head and a white throat with faint dots or streaks. The black-chinned hummingbird is typically 3¼ to 4 inches (8.3 to 9.7 cm) in length, with a wingspan of about 4¼ inches (11 cm).

Dimorphism: Sexual yes, seasonal no

Lifespan: male: 3 to 5 years, female: 8 to 11 years

Breeding range: Much of the American west, as far north as British Columbia, Washington, Oregon, and California, extending eastward to western Montana, southwestern Wyoming, Colorado, Oklahoma, and northern Mexico.

Nesting: 4 to 8 feet (1 to 2 meters) above ground

Eggs: 1 to 3

Generations: 2 or 3

Migration or overwintering: These birds migrate south in winter to parts of the southwestern US and northern Mexico.

Nectar sources: Bee balm, columbine, coral honeysuckle, lantana, lupine, petunias, scarlet sage, trumpet vine

Fun fact: During migration, black-chinned hummingbirds can fly for 18 to 20 hours nonstop, allowing them to cross the Gulf of Mexico.

A female black-chinned hummingbird.

A male black-chinned nectar feeding on a hummingbird bush.

Broad-Tailed Hummingbird

Selasphorus platycercus

Description: The population trend has declined by 14 percent over the last 10 years. The broad-tailed hummingbird averages between 4 and 4½ inches (10 cm) in length with a wingspan of about 5 inches (10 cm). Their preferred habitats are open areas within forests, such as mountain meadows, forest edges, subalpine meadows, foothills, and montane valley woodlands. The common name derives from both sexes having a long, broad tail that extends beyond their wingtips. They are unmistakable. The male is characterized by its bright, iridescent rose-magenta gorget or throat patch. Their gorget appears metallic and gleams in the sun. Male broad-tailed hummingbirds have a metallic green back and crown, with a white breast, and have green or yellowish-brown flanks. Their tail displays a bit of rufous coloring. Females are generally larger than males, lacking a complete gorget, replaced with green or bronze spots on the throat. Its flanks are yellowish-brown. The female's tail feathers have a green central tail feather, with a rusty colored base, black in the middle, and tipped in white.

A female nectaring on a California fuchsia.

A male broad-tailed hummingbird.

Dimorphism: Sexual yes, seasonal no

Lifespan: male: 1½ years, female: 12 years

Breeding range: The mountainous regions of the western US, from eastern and central California, Nevada, Utah, Arizona, New Mexico, Colorado, and west Texas, and extends into Wyoming and southern Montana.

Nest: 4 to 20 feet (1 to 6 meters) above ground

Eggs: 2

Generations: 1

Migration or overwintering: Migrates to Mexico and Guatemala for the winter

Nectar sources: Agastache, bee balm, butterfly bush, cardinal flower, canna, columbine, coral bells, fireweed, foxglove, golden currant, honeysuckle, Indian pink, milkweed, salvia, trumpet vine, and zinnia.

Fun fact: Males perform dazzling aerial displays to win over a female by flying high, then diving towards the ground at high speeds before pulling up at the last moment, and also flying horizontally, producing a loud trilling sound with their wings.

Calliope Hummingbird

Selasphorus calliope

Description: The population trend is relatively stable, with some regional variations. The calliope hummingbird is the smallest bird in North America, with an average length of 3 inches (8 cm) and an average wingspan of 4 inches (10 cm). Their preferred habitats are open montane forests, mountain meadows, and willow and alder thickets during the breeding season. They may also be found in chaparral, lowland brushy areas, and semi-desert regions during migration and winter. The name comes from the Greek muse of eloquence and epic poetry. Males are characterized by vibrant magenta gorget feathers. These feathers can be flared, creating a whiskered effect, especially during courtship displays. They also sport a glossy green back and crown, white underparts, and a dark tail. Females are small, green-backed birds with whitish or cinnamon-buff underparts and a whitish throat, with white eye-ring and a short tail, with minimal rufous color. Their sides and flanks are cinnamon or deep cinnamon buff, and their femoral tufts are white.

A female calliope hummingbird searching for nectar.

Dimorphism: Sexual yes, seasonal no

Lifespan: male: up to 6 years, female: 5 to 6 years

Breeding range: Western North America, from southern British Columbia and Alberta south to Colorado and southern California.

Nest: 6 to 39 feet (2 to 12 meters) above ground

Eggs: 2

Generations: 1 or 2

Migration or overwintering: It migrates to the southwestern United States, Mexico, and Central America for winter.

Nectar sources: Agastache, bee balm, cardinal flower, columbine, coral bells, fireweed, foxglove, California fuchsia, golden currant, honeysuckle, Indian paintbrush, indian pink, milkweed, petunia, salvia, trumpet gilia, trumpet vine, zinnia.

Fun fact: The calliope hummingbird undertakes an annual round trip of approximately 5,000 miles.

A male calliope hummingbird.

Ruby-Throated Hummingbird

Archilochus colubris

Description: From 1970 to the early 2000s, the population increased. However, from 2004 to the present, the population has decreased by as much as 17%; yet, it's still the most populous hummingbird species. But we can help improve the population by adding backyard feeders (and not spraying pesticides). Yes, these feeders make a difference! Keeping well-tended feeders and growing nectar-rich tubular flowers is paramount to protecting the ruby-throated hummingbird. A small bird, it's about 3 to 3¾ inches (8 to 10 cm) long, with a wingspan of 4 to 4¾ inches (10 cm). Their preferred habitats are open woodlands, forest edges, meadows, and gardens with lots of red to orange, tubular-shaped flowers. I look forward to the annual spring migration through my home garden. It's often said that when the native columbine is in bloom, that's when ruby-throated hummingbirds will arrive. These two species—the hummingbird and plant—have coevolved to synchronize their arrival in spring.

Males have ruby-red feathers around their gorgets. Their back and crown are a bright emerald or

A male ruby-throated on scarlet bee balm.

golden-green with white underbodies, while their wings are near black, and tail feathers are pointed and dark, often appearing forked. Females lack the red throat patch of the male and have a slender body and round tail, with a metallic green back and crown, and a white throat.

Dimorphism: Sexual yes, seasonal no

Lifespan: male: 3 to 5 years, female: 4 to 7

Breeding range: Eastern US and south-central and southeastern Canada. The ruby-throated hummingbird is the only hummingbird that breeds east of the Mississippi River.

Nest: 10 to 40 feet (3 to 12 meters) above ground. (No wonder I've never found one!)

Eggs: 1 to 2, rarely 3

Generations: 1 to 3

Migration or overwintering: The ruby-throated hummingbird may fly directly across the Gulf of Mexico to follow the coastal Gulf region. Depending on how far north they are migrating from, some ruby-throated hummingbirds, such as those summering in Canada, may winter along the Gulf Coast, parts of the southern East Coast, or at the tip of Florida. Ruby-throated hummingbirds primarily winter in southern Mexico, Central America, and Panama.

Nectar sources: Agastache, azalea, bee balm, cardinal flower, columbine, coral bells, coral honeysuckle, some cuphea, lantana, jewelweed, penstemon, phlox, rhododendron, salvia, trumpet creeper, trumpet honeysuckle.

Fun fact: The ruby-throated hummingbird weighs little more than a penny, but it can make the 500-mile journey across the Gulf of Mexico in less than a day!

A female ruby-throated hummer on scarlet sage.

A female ruby-throated hummingbird on an azure-blue sage stem.

Rufous Hummingbird

Selasphorus rufus

Description: Some estimate that rufous populations have experienced a 65% decline from 1970 to 2019. Rufous hummingbirds average 2¾ to 3½ inches (7 to 9 cm) in length, with a wingspan from 3 to 4¼ inches (8 to 11 cm). Their preferred habitats are open woodlands and coniferous forests with abundant shrubs for breeding. They are also found in forest edges, stream sides, and meadows, and are often present in parks and residential areas. The word "rufous" comes from the Latin *rufus*, meaning red or reddish. The rufous hummingbird is characterized by its distinctive rufous coloring. Males sport bright, iridescent red gorget, rusty-orange back and sides, and white breast. Some males may also have some green on their backs and crowns. Females are a dull bronze-green above with rufous flanks and a rufous base to the tail.

Dimorphism: Sexual yes, seasonal no

Lifespan: male: 3 to 5 years, female: 8 to 9 years

Breeding range: Rufous Hummingbirds are found in western North America, breeding in areas from southern Alaska through British Columbia and the Pacific Northwest to California, and wintering in Mexico.

A male rufous hummingbird.

A female rufous seeking nectar.

Nest: Averages between 10 and 20 feet (3 to 6 meters) high.

Eggs: 2 to 3

Generations: 1

Migration or overwintering: Rufous Hummingbirds undertake a long-distance migration, traveling from breeding grounds in Alaska and northwest Canada to wintering sites in Mexico, following a coastal route north in spring and returning through the Rocky Mountains in fall.

Nectar sources: Agastache, abutilon, azalea, bee balm, bleeding heart, cardinal flower, columbine, coral bells, some cuphea, fireweed, foxglove, California fuchsia, golden currant, honeysuckle, Indian paintbrush, Indian pink, lupine, milkweed, penstemon, petunia, salvia, trumpet gilia, trumpet vine, zinnia

Fun fact: undertake an incredibly long migration for their size, roughly a 3,900-mile journey from Alaska to Mexico!

Rufous hummingbirds are some of the larger species of hummers.

CHAPTER

4

Bees

One experiences fear or fascination or both when witnessing bees flit from flower to flower, but tasting the results of their pollination makes even the fearful satisfied—the crunch of almonds in granola, topped with golden honey, and the added sweetness of fresh peaches—there's nothing better, and all of it is made possible by bees. Did you know that the honeybee is the primary pollinator for commercial almond production? Without managed honeybees, almond yields would be radically reduced.

There are approximately 4,000 native bee species north of Mexico. Along with the introduced

A Halictus sweat bee feeding on a yellow calendula flower.

European honeybee, *Apis mellifera*, aka the western honeybee, these animals pollinate flowers, fruits, and veggies. (Would we even exist without them?)

Bees are grouped in seven families: Andrenidae, Apidae, Colletidae, Halictidae, Megachilidae, Melittidae, and Stenotritidae. The bee families Melittidae and Stenotritidae are not covered, as Melittidae is very rare in the US and Canada, and the Stenotritidae family is endemic to Australia. The remaining five families represent the majority of bee diversity north of Mexico, although the exact species within each family varies geographically. This book focuses on the ones we commonly find in our gardens—bumblebees, carpenter bees, honeybees, leafcutter bees, and mason bees.

A leafcutter bee with pollen.

How Bees Pollinate Plants

With hairs covering their bodies, bees are the most efficient pollinators. Female bees seek nectar, and when feeding, their hairs pick up pollen.

Some bees, like the honeybee, collect pollen in specialized structures on their legs called corbiculae, which are more commonly known as pollen baskets. Pollen baskets are specialized structures located on the lower part of the hind leg. The structures are smooth, hairless depressions with rows of long, curved hairs, essentially serving as receptacles to hold pollen for transport. When the female honeybee collects pollen, she packs pollen into her baskets, using a combination of her legs and saliva to transport it back to the hive. Pollen is stored in the hive cells, often near the brood.

Not all female bees have pollen baskets on their hind legs. Other bees use different methods to collect and transport pollen. The leafcutter and mason bees have scopa hairs on their abdomens instead of corbiculae on their hind legs, or, as with the carpenter bee, their pollen-collecting scopa hairs are located on their hind legs. Still other bees, such as those in the Colletidae family, carry pollen internally in their crops (a specialized part of a bee's digestive system, also known as the honey sac). Using their legs and saliva, they often form pollen into a ball for transport. Most bees can be categorized into two types of female pollen preferences: generalists and specialists.

A resin bee with pollen.

A honeybee with full pollen baskets.

Generalist Bees

Generalist bees, also known as polylectic bees, forage on a broad range of flowering plants for nectar and pollen. As such, they are crucial pollinators contributing to ecosystem health. Honeybees are a well-known example of generalist bees, as they forage on a wide variety of flowers.

Generalist bees can be found in several bee families, including Apidae, which encompasses honeybees, bumblebees, and carpenter bees, as well as others. The Halictidae family, known as sweat bees, and many species in the Megachilidae family, commonly referred to as leafcutter and mason bees, are also generalists.

Specialist Bees

Specialist bees, known as monolectic or oligolectic bees, are restricted to a much narrower range of plant species for pollen and nectar. Monolectic bees collect pollen from a single plant species. For example, the mining bee, *Andrena carolina*, is a specialist on blueberries. It is estimated that 20% to 45% of native bees are pollen specialists, seeking pollen from a single genus or species of plants. Without specific specialist pollinator bees, the plant doesn't reproduce. If these bees are removed, the plant dies. Many native specialist bees pollinate flowers that provide the foods we eat, such as squashes, pumpkins, gourds, and the annual sunflowers. In almost all food crops, native bees are the primary pollinators or significantly supplement the activity of honeybees. Even crops that don't rely on a pollinator will have a higher yield if bees visit them.

Oligolectic bees are specialized, but will forage from a few closely related plant species, often within the same plant family. For example, our native simple mining bee, *Andrena simplex*, forages within the Asteraceae family (asters), particularly on *Solidago* spp. (goldenrods), and *Symphyotrichum* spp. (ex-asters).

In addition to the two groups of pollinators, there are two additional adaptations—long-tongued and short-tongued bees.

Long-Tongued Bees

The familiar bumblebees, carpenter bees, and honeybees in the Apidae family, and mason bees and leafcutter bees in the Megachilidae family, are known to be long-tongued bees. The longer tongues of these bees allow them to access nectar from flowers with deep corolla tubes. The corolla tube is the part of the flower formed by the fusion of petals. Their long tongues allow them to reach nectar at the base of the flowers, picking up pollen as they feed, thereby pollinating the plant. Examples of flowers visited by long-tongued bees include foxgloves, honeysuckle, columbine, penstemons, and salvia.

Short-Tongued Bees

The bee families of the Andrenidae, Colletidae, and Halictidae are categorized as short-tongued bees. In contrast to the long-tongued bees, short-tongued bees seek nectar and pollen from open, easily accessible flowers within easy reach, such as asters, daisies, sunflowers, and yarrow, plus others with a landing pad and accessible corolla.

A short-tongued green sweat bee nectaring on Puget Sound gumweed.

Bumblebees extend their long tongues to reach nectar when visiting flowers.

A row of painted honeybee hives.

Sociability and Bees

Eusocial bees, such as bumblebees, stingless bees, and the honeybee, live in a caste system in which they form colonies with a clear division of roles. Eusociality is a complex form of social organization that involves cooperative brood care, overlapping generations within a colony, and division of labor around reproduction, with some individuals (the "workers") giving up their own reproduction to care for the offspring of other individuals (the "queen").

Solitary bees live and reproduce individually. Each female is responsible for building and provisioning her own solitary nest for her offspring and laying eggs. Some carpenter bees, *Xylocopa* spp., are examples. Most native bees are solitary and often nest underground; many are too small to be identified without the aid of a magnifying device.

Subsocial bees live and reproduce where the female bee cares for her offspring. This differs from solitary bees, which don't care for their young at all, and from social bees, which live in colonies with a division of labor. Subsocial bees represent an evolutionary step between solitary and social behavior. The small carpenter bee, a member of the genus *Ceratina*, is an example. They may share nests and sometimes cooperate in brood care, but lack the complex caste systems found in highly social bees.

Solitary red mason bees.

Communal bees are a type of bee where multiple females of the same generation share a nest, but each female constructs and provides for her own brood cells. An example is the sweat bee, *Agapostemon virescens*.

Quasi-social living occurs when multiple female bees emerge simultaneously from their nest. The female bee lays her eggs and provisions the nest. These females continue to share the nest and cooperate in caring for their young, but don't have a distinct worker caste system. The defining feature of quasi-sociality is the presence of cooperative brood care in which females in a single generation share a common nest.

The Andrenidae Family
(Mining Bees)

Subfamilies: Andreninae, Oxaeinae, Panurginae

Description: Mining bees are often confused with honeybees. Mining bees are ground-nesting solitary bees; however, females of many species may nest near each other, forming large aggregations. Mining bees dig burrows straight down in the ground to create nests, excavate tunnels in the soil, and appear to "mine" the ground. They line their nests with a waterproof substance secreted by the female to protect her progeny from soil moisture and bacteria. You'll find mining bees hovering close to the ground.

Each spring, I will get calls or texts about these amazing bees. People are fearful at first, but I assure them that mining bees are not aggressive. Mining bees are important early pollinators, often specialized pollinators. They are small to medium in size (from ⅓ to ¾ inch [7 to 18 mm] in length), characterized by dark coloration, and sometimes featuring banding.

Miner bees are short-tongued, making them suited for foraging on flowers with shallow or short corollas. Generalists favor early-spring ephemerals and early-blooming fruit trees. Specialists favor later-blooming asters, sunflowers, and goldenrods.

A female dawn mining bee entering her nest.

Bearded Miner Bee

Andrena barbilabris

Family: Andrenidae; Subfamily: Andrenidae

Description: The bearded miner bee appears to be common and widespread in its habitat. Bearded miner bees are strongly associated with sandy habitats and often nest in aggregations on south-facing banks or slopes. Other habitats include coastal dunes, gardens, and woodlands, as well as brownfield sites, provided the soil is sandy and wildflowers are present. They are typically active in the spring, with a flight period from March to June. It's a medium-size bee, with females typically measuring around ½ inch (11 mm) in length, and males smaller and more slender. Females are characterized by reddish-brown hairs on the thorax and distinct white bands on the abdomen. Males often appear silvery due to long pale hairs on the thorax.

A bearded miner bee in its usual sandy habitat.

This bearded miner bee nest is sited between paving bricks.

Lifespan: A few weeks

Geographic range: Southern Canada and northern US

Foraging range: About ¼ mile (300 to 500 meters)

Short-tongued

Generalists

Favored plants: Angelica, blackberries, carrots, cinquefoils, cow parsley, dandelions, dill, fennel, parsley, Queen Anne's lace, willows

Pollen collection method: Via a large scopa on their hind legs and the back sides of their thorax

Sociability: Solitary, but may build individual nest in close proximity to other nests

Fun fact: While both males and females visit flowers for nectar, only females actively collect pollen to provision their nests.

The Apidae Family (Honeybees, Bumblebees, and Carpenter Bees)

Subfamilies: Apinae, Bombinae, Xylocopinae, plus eight others

Description: The bees belonging to the Apidae family are an incredibly diverse group, comprising the well-known bumblebees, carpenter bees, and honeybees. There are over 5,900 species worldwide, with approximately 1,000 species found north of Mexico. Bees in the Apidae family share key characteristics, such as long tongues and the ability to carry pollen in similar ways. They vary from solitary to highly social.

Honeybees are considered eusocial, meaning they form perennial, large colonies, and are also known for their complex hive structures and honey production. This may not be news to you. However, did you know that bumblebees are also eusocial, albeit with smaller colonies and seasonal activity? Some carpenter bees are considered semi-social bees, exhibiting some cooperative brood care, but not the full range found in eusocial species.

A large portion of bees in the Apidae family are solitary, where the female builds her own nest, provisions it with food, and lays her eggs without social interaction.

Apidae bees are vital pollinators in both natural habitats, including our gardens, and in agricultural ecosystems. The honeybee, for example, contributes up to $5.4 billion in agricultural productivity in the US.

A tropical carpenter bee drilling holes in wood.

Honeybee

Apis mellifera

Family: Apidae; Subfamily: Apinae

Description: Although native to Africa, Europe, and western Asia, honeybees, often referred to as the European honeybee, or more recently, the western honeybee, were introduced to the US in 1622 by British colonists establishing the Jamestown colony in Virginia. As pollinators, honeybees are a billion-dollar industry, as they are crucial for agriculture and ecosystems. But over the past several decades, honeybee populations have experienced declines and recoveries. Currently, managed honeybee colonies continue to face ongoing challenges and declines in colony numbers, especially those north of Mexico. The losses for honeybees mirror the decline of other pollinators—pesticide use being the culprit. As of April 1, 2024, there were reportedly 2.71 million colonies, with each colony containing between 10,000

Honeybees visiting some red clover.

and 60,000 bees. Honeybees exist in a wide range of habitats where there are flowering plants to feed on nectar and to carry pollen to their hive. In addition to managed hives, honeybees nest in gardens, grasslands, and woodlands, where they typically build nests in tree cavities and rock crevices. Honeybees are about ½ inch (12 mm) long, honey-colored, brown with some black markings. The abdomen is striped, and the honeybee has a heart-shaped face. Don't let that sweet face fool you; if you get too close to their hive, the female worker bees will defend their habitat. It's best to stay clear of hives, whether managed or wild. Male honeybees have very large eyes that touch at the top of their head, which are better at spotting the queen in flight in order to mate with her. These drones are slightly larger and stockier than female worker bees and lack a stinger. Instead, drones have a modified ovipositor, an organ used for mating with the queen. Female honeybees have smaller, separated eyes and a stinger.

Lifespan: The lifespan of a honeybee varies depending on its role in the colony and the time of year. The female worker bees typically live for 4 to 6 weeks during the summer, while those born in the fall can live for up to 4 to 6 months. The male drone bees typically live for about 4 to 6 weeks. The queen bees can live for up to 2 to 3 years.

Geographic range: throughout North America

Foraging range: 1 to 2 miles (1½ to 3 km)

Long-tongued

Generalists

Favored plants: Bee balm, borage, clover, coneflowers, lavender, goldenrod, sunflowers, and many more.

Pollen collection method: Pollen is stored on their hind legs, in pollen baskets called corbicula.

Sociability: Honeybees are eusocial, highly social in fact!

Fun fact: Honeybees communicate through intricate dances, pheromones, and vibrations. The most well-known method is the waggle dance, where returning foragers communicate the location and quality of food sources.

Honeybee queens are larger than the other female worker bees. In this commercial hive, the queen bee has been marked with a pink dot.

The Honeybee Caste System

The western honeybee, *Apis mellifera*, also known as the European honeybee, has the most well-known example of a caste system among bees. When a honeybee is born, its social stratification is set.

The honeybee goes through a complete metamorphosis—egg, larva, pupa, and adult. The development time from egg to an adult varies slightly depending on the bee's role in the caste-system hive.

It takes about 16 days to make a new queen. For a female worker bee, it takes about 21 days to develop from an egg to an adult bee. For male drones, it takes around 24 days. The varying development time is a combination of factors related to their roles within the colony, including diet, cell size, and genetic pathways. Here's a breakdown of each caste.

The Queen Bee

To make a queen bee, nurse bees exclusively feed a fertilized female bee royal jelly, leading to a large size, longer lifespan, and reproductive capacity compared to other female worker bees.

Within days after emerging as a queen bee, mating flights begin. On sunny, warm afternoons, the queen bee will leave the hive to fly to a Drone Congregation Area (DCA) where drones from many colonies gather. During these flights, the queen bee mates mid-air with up to 20 or more drones. The entire mating process with each drone takes just a few seconds. After mating, the drone dies, and the queen stores the sperm in her spermatheca for later use. After the queen bee has mated and returns to the hive, she typically starts laying eggs within two or three days. The queen bee resembles the female worker bees but has an enlarged abdomen.

The queen bee determines whether to fertilize an egg based on the type of cell she is laying it in. The larger cells are designated for the male drone eggs. Smaller cells are for the female worker bees. To know the cell size for laying purposes, the queen uses her legs for measurement.

Worker Bees

Queen and female worker bees are developed from fertilized eggs, inheriting the genetic material of the queen and the mated drone. All fertilized eggs have the potential to develop into either a female,

specifically a queen, or a worker. Female worker bees are typically sterile, meaning they cannot mate and lay fertilized eggs. However, they can lay unfertilized eggs, which develop into male bees, drones. If a colony loses its queen, some worker bees may develop functional ovaries and start laying eggs, but these eggs will always be unfertilized and develop into drones. In essence, the initial fertilization of the egg determines the bee's sex. For the female larvae, the amount of royal jelly they consume during development determines whether they will become queens or worker bees. Female worker bees receive a diet of royal jelly for the first three days, followed by a mixture of honey and pollen.

Worker bees play several key roles within the hive, including caring for the young, building and maintaining the honeycomb, foraging for food and water, and defending the colony. The age of the worker bee determines the tasks they perform.

Age 1 to 3 days. Newly emerged nurse worker bees focus on cleaning the cells within the hive, preparing the cells for the queen's eggs, food, and storage.

Age 3 to 14 days. As they mature, female bees become nurse bees, during which they feed older larvae and secrete royal jelly for the younger larvae.

Age 18 to 21 days. Worker bees have four pairs of wax glands located on the underside of their abdomen. These glands secrete beeswax, which is used to build and maintain the honeycomb structure of the hive. At this age, as the worker bees can't perform their tasks, caring for the honeycomb, they stand guard from unwelcome guests, such as bees from another hive trying to steal food reserves.

Age Over 21 days. Older worker bees transition to foraging, collecting nectar, pollen, water, and propolis, also known as "bee glue," which is a resinous substance that honeybees produce by mixing tree sap with their secretions. Bees use it to seal cracks in the hive, smooth rough surfaces, and protect the hive against invaders.

Drone Bees

Drones are male bees whose primary role is to mate with the queen. They don't have stingers and are generally larger than worker bees, but smaller than the queen. Male drones develop from unfertilized eggs laid by the queen, making them haploid organisms, meaning they inherit only one set of chromosomes, those from the queen. Male drones also receive royal jelly during the larval stage.

The amount of royal jelly a female honebee larva receives determines whether it will be a queen or a worker.

Eastern Bumblebee

Bombus impatiens

Family: Apidae; Subfamily: Apinae

Description: The population trend of the eastern bumblebee is considered stable and may even be increasing. This is good news; however, not all *Bombus* spp. are doing so well. The American bumblebee (*Bombus pensylvanicus*) has been reported to have declined by up to 89%. The Franklin's bumblebee (*Bombus franklini*) is listed as endangered, as is the rusty-patched bumblebee (*Bombus affinis*), and in the US, the western bumblebee (*Bombus occidentalis*) experienced a 40% decline in the last 20 years.

An eastern bumblebee nectaring on bee balm.

The eastern bumblebee is characterized by its dense, fuzzy body, with a predominantly yellow thorax and first abdominal segment, while the remaining abdominal segments are black. A key feature is the black patch in the middle of the thorax, between the wing bases. Males can be distinguished by a yellow patch on their face.

While typically ground-nesters, preferring existing rodent holes or other pre-existing cavities, occasionally, the *Bombus impatiens* builds nests above ground, in dense vegetation, such as clump grasses, and occasionally in birdhouses.

The eastern bumblebee varies in size depending on the caste, with distinct groups of bees within a colony having specialized roles and physical differences. The largest eastern bumblebee is the queen, measuring between ⅔ and 9⁄10 inch (17 and 23 mm) in length. Female workers are smaller, measuring between ⅓ and ⅔ inch (8 and 16 mm). Male drones measure between ½ and ¾ inch (12 and 18 mm).

Bumblebees have an annual lifecycle, during which a single queen lives and is active for one season. The lifecycle is continuous, though, as each foundress queen initiates a new colony independently. She finds a new nest in which to overwinter, emerging from hibernation in the spring. At this time, she will spend a few weeks foraging and searching for a new nest location. The queen bee is looking for existing cavities, such as grass clumps or existing rodent holes.

They are one of the most common and earliest emerging bumblebees in the spring through fall.

Lifespan: Queens live for about one year. Female worker bees live 4 to 6 weeks, depending on the season. During summer months, they may live for about six weeks, but in the winter, they can live up to three months. Male drones live for a few weeks and only to mate with their queen.

Geographic range: Widespread and adaptable throughout much of eastern North America

Foraging range: between ⅓ and 1 mile (500 and 1,750 meters)

Long-tongued

Generalists

Favored plants: asters, bee balm, coneflowers, goldenrod, lavender, and milkweed.

Pollen collection method: uses their hairy bodies and their corbiculae, pollen baskets, located on their hind legs.

Sociability: Eusocial

Fun fact: The common bumblebee uses a foraging strategy called "traplining", meaning they visit their food sources in the same order every time, which helps them be more efficient, especially in new areas. They establish these "traplines" by systematically exploring and then sticking to a preferred route.

Eastern Carpenter Bee

Xylocopa virginica

Family: Apidae; Subfamily: Xylocopinae

Description: The eastern carpenter bee population is considered stable. *Xylocopa virginica* are a large, robust bee, often mistaken for bumblebees, but their shiny, black abdomen distinguishes them—what I call a shiny heinie! The eastern carpenter bee measures between ¾ and 1 inch (2 and 2.5 cm) in length. It prefers habitats with both flowers for food and wood for nesting. Specifically, they excavate tunnels in wood, such as dead trees, stumps, logs, and other wooden structures, such as unpainted wood, fences, decks, and even buildings. For homeowners, many dread the carpenter bee breeding season, as they are likely to build a nest within the wood of your personal property. While research suggests carpenter bees prefer unpainted wood, they never seem to mind our painted back porch! The eastern carpenter bee

A female eastern carpenter bee nectar-robbing a nasturtium.

This Eastern carpenter bee's nest was built in an old wood pallet.

has a fuzzy thorax, with colors varying from yellow to orange or white. Male carpenter bees have white or yellow markings on their face, while females have a completely black head.

Lifespan: The eastern carpenter bee has no queen, and female worker bees generally live for one year, some even longer. The male drones typically die in the spring after mating.

Geographic range: Eastern, central, and southern parts of the United States, extending north into Canada

Foraging range: Up to 1 mile (1.62 km)

Long-tongued, but due to the large size of carpenter bees, many resort to nectar-robbing on flowers with long or narrow corollas. These bees cut a slit at the base of the flower to access nectar. In doing so, they avoid coming into contact with pollen, thereby preventing pollination from occurring. This can affect the reproduction success of certain plants. Watch and enjoy these nectar-robbers, and know there are many other insects pollinating these flowers.

Generalists

Favored plants: Garden crops including eggplant, tomato, passion fruit, and cucurbits.

Pollen collection method: *Xylocopa* spp. transport pollen primarily on their hind legs. And through sonication, pollen is collected on their underside, which they then redistribute to their legs. Additionally, a significant portion is also ingested and stored in their crops.

Sociability: *Xylocopa* spp. are neither entirely solitary nor fully eusocial, depending on the availability of resources. When nesting resources are abundant, individual females tend to nest solitarily. When resources are limited, they will cooperate and share a nesting site.

Fun fact: Eastern carpenter bees only leave their nests on warm days.

The Colletidae Family (Cellophane, Plaster Bees)

Subfamilies: Colletinae, Diphaglossinae, Xeromelissinae, Hylaeinae, Euryglossinae

Description: Cellophane, or plaster, bees are so called because they line their next cells with a mucosal secretion that dries to form a cellophane-like lining. They are often regarded as the most primitive bees, due to characteristics they share with spheciform wasps, thought to be the ancestors of bees. There is no definitive report on the population trend of the Colletidae family; however, some Colletidae species may be experiencing decline. For example, the *Colletes wolfi* and *Colletes sierrensis* are considered at risk.

Colletes are important pollinators for spring crops. The Colletinae family is a ground nester, sometimes in aggregations with sufficient numbers to resemble a bee village, yet no shared labor is involved. Or they nest in hollow cavities; in each case, the female provides provisions to their brood with balls of pollen and nectar transported by the legs and mouthparts.

The Colletidae bee family is diverse in size, with polyester bees in the genus *Colletes* measuring between ⅓ and ⅔ inches (7 and 15 mm). The yellow-faced bee in the genus *Hylaeus*, measuring between ⅕ and ⅓ inch (5 and 7 mm), and the larger Colletid bees, with some found in the subfamily Diphaglossinae, can reach up to almost 1 inch (24 mm). Colletes tend to be very hairy compared to other bees of similar size. Many have pale bands of light-colored hair on their abdomen.

Several Colletes species specialize in plants in the Asteraceae family.

A plasterer bee resting on a leaf.

Unequal Cellophane Bees

Colletes inaequalis

Family: Colletidae; Subfamily: Colletinae

Description: *Colletes inaequalis* was only described in 2016, so there is no long-term population trend estimate; however, short-term trends since that time appear to be relatively stable. The unequal cellophane bee is small, with females measuring between ⅓ and ½ inch (10 and 13 mm) and males measuring between ⅓ and ⅖ inch (9 and 10 mm). The unequal prefers open areas with sparse vegetation and well-drained soil, particularly in urban and suburban areas. They often nest in aggregations in areas like lawns, parks, and cemeteries. These bees are among the first to emerge in spring and are known for their large, ground-nesting aggregations.

Male unequal cellophane bees surround a lone female.

Unequal cellophane bees are ground-nesting bees.

Lifespan: Females typically live four to five weeks. Males typically die after mating.

Geographic range: Eastern US and southeast Canada

Foraging range: up to ⅓ mile (600 meters)

Short-tongued

Generalists

Favored plants: Apple, blueberry, chokecherry, eastern redbud, gooseberry, red maple, serviceberry, viburnum, wild cherry, and willow, as well as blue squills, crocus, dandelion, and snowdrops.

Pollen collection method: Colletes collect and transport pollen to their brood via their scopa, located on their hind legs.

Sociability: Solitary

Fun fact: Unequal cellophane bees are considered a true sign of spring in the eastern US, as they are among the earliest pollinators to emerge in spring, often appearing when there's still snow on the ground, particularly in the northeast.

The Halictidae Family (Sweat Bees)

Subfamilies: Halictinae, Nomioidinae, Nomiinae, Rophitinae

Description: Halictidae get their common name from their tendency to be attracted to perspiration and lick sweat from humans and other animals to obtain salts and nutrients. Sweat bees are abundant in North America, with over 500 species in the US alone. These bees are not restricted to specific habitats, inhabiting diverse environments from arctic regions to various terrestrial locations.

These beautiful bees are noted for their distinct colors ranging from metallic blue, brown, or purple to black or brown. They range from ⅓ to ⅔ inch (7 to 14 mm) long.

Sweat bees are mostly ground nesting, digging deep, vertical burrows in flat or sloping soil, preferring soil or sand. They can be solitary or live in eusocial colonies with distinct castes. Sweat bees are important pollinators for agricultural crops.

There are nearly 4,500 species in the Halictidae family.

Pure Green Sweat Bee

Augochlora pura

Family: Halictidae; Subfamilies: Rophitinae, Nomiinae, Nomioidinae, (especially) Halictinae.

Description: The *Augochlora pura* is a small, vibrant, shiny green bee common in the eastern US, in most of its range, but tends to be a deep metallic blue in Florida. The exact causes for this color variation are not entirely understood. The bright green coloring distinguishes it from other, duller metallic green sweat bees, such as the common furrow bee, *Lasioglossum morio*. Males and females are similar in appearance, but males may have darker mandibles and a slightly bluish hue. *Augochlora pura* builds its nests in rotting wood, under loose bark on older trees, and often under fallen logs in forests. The pure green sweat bee's preferred habitat is in shady hardwood forests and nearby open areas, such as brush and pastures, with abundant flowers. It's about ⅓ inch (8 mm) long. Both sexes have been observed licking sweat from human skin, likely seeking salts and other nutrients.

These sweat bees have a shiny green color.

Pure green sweat bees collect pollen using scopae on their hind legs.

Lifespan: Females live long enough to complete nine to 12 nests. There are typically two to three generations per year, and females from the final generation overwinter to reproduce the following year, either alone or in groups. Males soon die after mating.

Geographic range: Maine to Minnesota and south to Texas and Florida, and as far north as Quebec

Foraging range: Up to ⅓ mile (600 meters)

Short-tongued

Generalists

Favored plants: Asters, buttonbush, chickweed, Columbine, hydrangeas, goldenrods, milkweeds, spiderwort, verbena, walnut

Pollen collection method: Via scopae on their hind legs

Sociability: Some species are solitary, others are communal, with multiple females sharing a single nest entrance. The female still constructs and provisions her brood cells.

Fun fact: It has been proposed that the pure green sweat bee, *Augochlora pura*, is one of the few animal pollinators for the walnut tree, *Juglans regia*.

The Megachilidae Family

Subfamilies: Fideliinae, Pararhophitinae, Lithurginae, Megachilinae

Description: These families of native bees are commonly known as large leafcutter bees. I don't often see them, but I cherish sightings of their perfectly cut circles from leaves, which they use in constructing their nests. They are particularly beautiful on my native redbud, *Cercis canadensis* 'Flame Thrower', with brightly colored orange and red leaves, and hence colorful leaf fragments that seal their nests. These fragments also create partitions between brood cells and line the outer walls of the cells. If you watch closely, you might witness a female leafcutter flying back to her nest, clasping a piece of leaf like a witch riding a broomstick.

About 242 native species exist, plus the alfalfa leafcutter bee (*Megachile rotundata*), introduced in the 1930s for its agricultural services and now naturalized in North America. While a wide range of colors and patterns exists, they often appear black, brown, or metallic (such as green, bronze, or blue) with contrasting pale or yellow bands across their abdomens. Bees in the Megachilidae family have stout bodies and range in size from ¼ to 1 inch long.

Most are considered generalists, visiting larger flowers in the bean and aster families, as well as other flowers. Leafcutter bees are essential pollinators of many wildflowers and of those flowers found in our cultivated gardens.

These bees are generally not aggressive and only sting if directly provoked.

A Megachile leaf-cutter bee nectaring on a crown daisy.

Patchwork Leafcutter Bee

Megachile centuncularis

Family: Megachilidae; Subfamily: Megachilidae

Description: The population trend is considered stable. Leafcutter bees are cavity nesters and will nest in pre-existing holes, making it easy to provide them with nesting opportunities. Either a bee hotel or leaving hollow-stemmed flower stalks up at least 8 inches or more, such as sumac, raspberry stalks, or thistles. The patchwork leafcutter bee has a very limited foraging range. Place leafcutter bee boxes near an abundance of plant life. Measuring between ⅕ and ⅘ inch (5 to 21 mm) long.

A patchwork leafcutter bee on a Marguerite daisy.

Patchwork leafcutter bees can make good use of bee bungalows and similar structures.

Lifespan: Females will live for a few weeks; males die after mating.

Geographic range: throughout North America

Foraging range: up to 300 feet (90 meters)

Long-tongued

Generalists

Favored plants: Fleabane, butterfly pea, cat's ear, knapweeds, thistles, and various members of the pea family, such as prairie clover and wild pea.

Pollen collection method: Megachile bees collect and transport pollen using a dense mat of long hairs on the underside of their abdomen called a scopa, or pollen brush.

Sociability: Solitary, but they like to nest near each other, making manmade structures desirable and educational.

Fun fact: The patchwork leafcutter bee uses saliva to glue pieces of leaves together, forming individual cells within its nest to house its eggs and provide a food source.

Blue Orchard Bee, Mason Bee

Osmia lignaria

Family: Megachilidae; Subfamily: Megachilinae

Description: The population trend of our native *Osmia lignaria* is declining. A long-term study in the mid-Atlantic indicated a significant annual decline, potentially linked, in part, to the introduction of non-native *Osmia* spp., including *O. taurus* and *O. cornifrons*, which may outcompete native species and transmit diseases. These small bees prefer to nest in pre-existing cavities, making it easy to provide suitable nesting sites for them—either a bee hotel or leaving hollow-stemmed flower stalks up at least 8 inches or more, such as sumac, raspberry stalks, or thistles. The mason bee measures between 1/5 and 4/5 inch (5 to 21 mm) in length. Mason bees are typically active in early spring for a period of 6 to 8 weeks.

A blue orchard bee resting on a salmonberry leaf.

This in-progress nest already includes pollen and nectar gathered by a blue orchard mason bee.

Lifespan: Females live about a month; males die shortly after mating.

Geographic range: All states except Alaska, Florida, and Hawaii; southern Canada

Foraging range: 200 to 300 feet (61 to 91 meters)

Long-tongued

Generalists

Favored plants: Almond, apples, cherry, mints, legumes

Pollen collection method: Megachile bees collect and transport pollen using a dense mat of long hairs on the underside of their abdomen called a scopa, or pollen brush.

Sociability: Solitary, but they like to nest near each other, making manmade structures desirable and educational.

Fun fact: Mason bees are very effective pollinators, even more so than honeybees. They are often mistaken for house flies due to their appearance, but they produce a buzzing sound rather than a humming sound.

Bee Bungalows for Blue Orchard, Mason, and Leafcutter Bees

When visiting gardens, parks, or arboretums, I'm sure you've encountered a native bee bungalow, also known as a bee hotel; perhaps you've one of your own or have wondered how to create one.

Mason and leafcutter bees are cavity-nesting insects. In the wild, they nest in hollow stems, tunnels, or holes formed by wood-boring insects. As such, gardener-made nesting sites are suitable for these solitary bees. The ideal hole size is 5⁄16 inch wide. Premade boxes are available. Just make sure the depth is at least 6 inches.

These native bee pollinators are crucial to our ecosystem, as they are up to three times more effective at pollinating flowers than the European honeybee and are gentle toward humans.

When adding native bee bungalows, it's better to host several small houses instead of one large bee hotel. Spread the nesting sites around, so if a predator penetrates one, it won't necessarily get to all of the bees.

Blue orchard bees, *Osmia lignaria*, are among the first to pollinate in the spring. Fuzzy with blue/green metallic color, about the size of a housefly, they are active from February to June and prefer to feed on nectar and pollen from fruit flowers, such as blueberry, apple, pear, peach, plum, plus others. Once the female chooses her nesting site, she begins collecting nesting materials and laying eggs. The female builds her chamber walls out of mud, clay, or other masonry-type materials—one of the important reasons to leave areas of your garden mulch-free!

Mason bees line their nesting tubes with pollen cakes to feed their developing larvae. Building the innermost wall of the nest requires approximately ten trips to collect mud. The female mason bee then closes off her nest tube with a cap of mud or clay. If you see these caps on the bee tubes, you should expect new mason bees to emerge the following spring.

Leafcutter bees, *Megachilidae* spp., are about the size of a honeybee with a fuzzy appearance and cream and black stripes on the abdomen. Active from May to November, they feed on nectar and pollen from fruits and vegetable flowers such as beans, blackberries, cucumbers, and tomatoes. The leafcutter bee also feeds on native wildflowers such as milkweed, liatris, asters, coneflower, blanket flower, sunflower, and more. Females gather pollen and nectar, lay eggs, and seal egg chambers with leaves or flower petals. You may have noticed circles cut from certain plants. These minor cuts do not harm the plants. Leafcutter bees wrap their eggs with these cut soft leaves or flower petals and cap their nest within the bee tubes with similar gatherings. If you see these caps on the bee tubes, often colorful, you should expect new leafcutter bees to emerge next spring and summer.

To make nesting efficient in my home garden, I built mud stations near the nesting sites by adding a saucer of clay. The mud station provides the mason bees with a readily available source of nest sealant, saving them time and energy and ensuring they can focus on their nesting activities.

Bee bungalows can be homemade or store-bought, modern or rustic, as long as they include the cavities these species need.

Tips for Siting a Bee Bungalow

Your bee bungalow can not only be practical for mason and leafcutter bee nesting, but it can also be a work of art and a conversation starter when sharing your garden with friends.

- Mount the bee bungalow about 5 feet above the ground, on structures such as a garage, shed, or mature tree. It's never a good idea to put a nail in a tree; when only a tree is available, it's best to securely hang the bee bungalow from the branch using string.
- Orient the bee tube entrance toward sunrise (east or southeast)
- Protect it from strong winds.
- When bees are active, refrain from spraying pesticides. (I never use pesticides in my home garden.)
- When bees are building their nests, refrain from removing or rearranging the materials they use for nesting.
- Surround the bee bungalow area with flowering plants for nectar and pollen.

Remove spent tubes once they are used to prevent diseases and pathogen buildup.

CHAPTER 5

Native Plant Profiles

Agastaches

Family: Lamiaceae (mint family); Genus: Agastache

Description: *Agastache* is pronounced a-guh-stash. Say it however you like, but be sure to include at least one or more (I like to plant at least three or more of a kind) in your pollinator garden. *Agastache* spp. are herbaceous perennials, typically with an erect growth habit. In addition to its tolerance to drought, it is also resistant to deer (although deer will eat anything if they are hungry enough!).

As a member of the mint family, *Agastache* spp. have aromatic scents like mint, licorice, or anise, and square stems, a hallmark of the mint family. There are 22 species native to North America. Well-drained soils are essential; wet feet, in poorly drained substrate, especially in winter, will result in a quick demise. If your soil is too moist or doesn't drain well, consider planting it in a raised bed or container.

An adult female calliope hummingbird filling up on nectar before fall migration.

Threadleaf or Giant Hyssop

Agastache rupestris

Description: Threadleaf hyssop is an upright, clump-forming pollinator plant with showy, fragrant, long-blooming flower spikes that bloom most of the summer. Colors range from white to blue and shades of red and purple. Native to the southwestern United States and Mexico.

Hardiness Zones: 5 to 8

Bloom Time: July to September

Size: 1½ feet to 2 feet tall by 1 to feet wide

Sun: Full to part shade

Water: Dry, average, well-drained soil, will not tolerate wet feet

Butterfly Larval Host: Buckeye butterfly

Wildlife Food Value: Butterflies, hummingbirds, short- and long-tongued bees

A female broad-tailed hummingbird enjoying *Agastache rupestris* nectar.

Anise Hyssop

Agastache foeniculum

Description: Typically found in prairies, plains, and fields, this upright, clump-forming perennial is a member of the mint family and is well-suited for the cultivated pollinator habitat. It blooms from mid-to late-summer with lavender to purple flowers in terminal spikes, with anise-scented foliage. It's an excellent, nectar-rich, bee plant, historically planted en masse to support apiaries. Native to much of North America.

Hardiness Zones: 4 to 10

Bloom Time: July to September

Size: 2 to 4 feet tall by 1½ to 3 feet wide

Sun: Full to part shade

Water: Dry, average, well-drained soil

Butterfly Larval Host: Buckeye butterfly

Wildlife Food Value: Butterflies, hummingbirds, short- and long-tongued bees

Anise hyssop is a fragrant perennial.

Hummingbird Mint

Agastache cana

Description: As the common name suggests, *A. cana* is a magnet to hummingbirds, as are all agastaches. A herbaceous wood-based perennial, with tubular, rose-pink to raspberry-pink, or even deep magenta flowers, that are sweetly fragrant, resembling the smell of chewing gum. Native to the southern US

Hardiness Zones: 5 to 9

Bloom Time: June to July

Size: 1½ to 3 feet tall by 1 to 2 feet wide

Sun: Full to part shade

Water: Dry to average

Butterfly Larval Host: No butterflies, some moths

Wildlife Food Value: Butterflies, hummingbirds, short- and long-tongued bees

Hummingbird mint can have brilliant magenta blooms.

Orange Hummingbird Mint

Agastache aurantiaca

Description: the orange hummingbird mint is orange, and it attracts hummingbirds—hence the name. Hummingbirds flock to the plant's stalks of tubular, nectar-rich flower spikes. And the color, oh that soft orange color, is so desirable; I submit that even orange haters (and I've known a few) would favor this plant. Native to the southwestern United States and northern Mexico.

Hardiness Zones: 5 to 9

Bloom Time: Midsummer to early fall

Size: 2 to 3 feet tall by 1½ to 2 feet wide

Sun: Full

Water: average

Butterfly Larval Host: No butterflies, some moths

Wildlife Food Value: Butterflies, hummingbirds, short- and long-tongued bees

Orange hummingbird mint usually has a softer orange color.

Aromatic Aster

Symphyotrichum oblongifolium

Description: A robust, star performer perennial, forming a compact, low-growing, dense mound with daisy-like, blue/purple flowers, and a cheery golden/yellow center, this aster's aromatic scent is released when foliage is crushed. It's an important fall-blooming flower, providing nectar and pollen well into October, or through first frost. Native to the northeastern and central United States and Canada.

Hardiness Zones: 3 to 8

Bloom Time: September through November

Size: 1 to 3 feet tall and wide

Sun: Full

Water: Dry, average, well-drained

Butterfly Larval Host: painted lady, pearl crescent, silvery checkerspot

Wildlife Food Value: Short- and long-tongued bees (especially the queen bumblebee)

Aromatic aster provides nectar and pollen through the first frost.

Blue Sky Aster

Symphyotrichum oolentangiense

Description: Having daisy-like flowers of blue with a sunshine-yellow disk, blue sky aster is an important September and October blooming flower, as are all the asters. They provide a rich nectar and pollen source to benefit fall pollinators. A rhizomatous perennial found at woodland edges, open woods, and prairies, it can be grown in a variety of soils. Native to the eastern United States and Canada.

Hardiness Zones: 3 to 8

Bloom Time: August to October

Size: 2 to 3 feet tall and 1½ to 2 feet wide

Sun: Full

Water: Dry, tolerates drought, average

Butterfly Larval Host: Pearl crescent, silvery checkerspot

Wildlife Food Value: Butterflies, hummingbirds, short- and long-tongued bees

The blue sky aster can handle drier spaces.

Heart-Leaved or Blue Wood Aster

Symphyotrichum cordifolium

Description: Blue wood aster can become somewhat weedy, but it is easy to pull. An herbaceous perennial native to rich, dry to moist woodlands, forest margins, fields, dry meadows, bluff bases, and stream banks, it has stems that are topped with dense, small-leaved panicles of daisy-like flowers, featuring violet or purple ray florets and yellow disk florets. Deadhead to limit self-seeding. Native to eastern and central North America.

Hardiness Zones: 3 to 8

Bloom Time: August to October

Size: 1 to 4 feet tall by 1 to 2 feet wide

Sun: Full to part shade

Water: Average, wet

Butterfly Larval Host: Pearl crescent

Wildlife Food Value: Butterflies, hummingbirds, short- and long-tongued bees

These flowers brighten partly shaded spots in the garden.

California Aster

Symphyotrichum chilense

Description: Expect California aster to spread aggressively by rhizomes and give this plant lots of room. Featuring daisy-like flowers in shades of blue, lavender, and purple, with yellow centers, California aster is native to coastal California and the Pacific Northwest.

Hardiness Zones: 6 to 10

Bloom Time: Midsummer to late fall

Size: 1 to 4 feet tall by 1 to 3 feet wide

Sun: Full to partial sun

Water: Average

Butterfly Larval Host: Checkerspot, crescent

Wildlife Food Value: Butterflies, hummingbirds, bumblebees, honeybees

Symphyotrichum chilense requires a lot of space.

Columbines

Family: Ranunculaceae (buttercup family); Genus: Aquilegia

Description: Columbines are known for their diversity of colors, shapes, and sizes. Perennial flowering plants known for their distinctive, spurred flowers and lobed foliage, there are numerous species and cultivars, offering a wide range of options for gardeners. In my home garden, I tend to stick to straight species, if I can find them, and leave those lovely cultivars for the gardenistas. Columbines are found in meadows and woodlands and thrive in my home garden. As a fan of self-seeders, I look forward to seeing where the happy accidents come up in the garden next spring. Did you know that it is said the ruby-throated hummingbird's arrival is when the columbine is in bloom?

Aquilegia canadensis has brilliant red flowers.

Wild Columbine, Canadian Columbine, or Red Eastern Columbine

Aquilegia canadensis

Description: With a unique architecture, spring flowers are characterized by their distinctive nodding red-and-yellow, bell-shaped flowers with long spurs. Don't let the delicate nature of columbine fool you; it can irritate the skin when handling. The self-seeding nature of this plant, causing it to show up in the most unusual places, gives me great delight. This plant is the only butterfly host plant for the columbine duskwing. Native to eastern North America.

Hardiness Zones: 3 to 8

Bloom Time: April to June

Size: 2 to 3 feet tall and 1 to 1½ feet wide

Sun: Full to part shade

Water: Average, well-drained

Butterfly Larval Host: Columbine duskywing

Wildlife Food Value: Hummingbirds, long-tongued bumblebees

Wild columbine blooms in spring.

Western Columbine

Aquilegia formosa

Description: Stunning scarlet red and soft yellow flowers bloom in late spring to early summer, forming bushy, large, upright clumps. Flowers are typically two inches across, featuring straight spurs and golden stamens. The indigenous peoples of California would gather the young foliage, before the columbine bloomed, to eat after boiling. Native to western North America including Alaska.

Hardiness Zones: 3 to 8

Bloom Time: April to August

Size: 1 to 3 feet tall by 8 inches to 2 feet wide

Sun: Full, part shade

Water: Average

Butterfly Larval Host: Columbine duskywing butterfly

Wildlife Food Value: Hummingbirds, long-tongued bees

Western columbine is a food source for hummingbirds and long-tongued bees.

Golden Columbine

Aquilegia chrysantha

Description: Golden columbine is a bushy, clump-forming perennial, native to canyons in damp places in the desert southwest and northern Mexico, with a disjunct population in southern Colorado, although the Colorado plants have shorter spurs and are sometimes referred to as *Aquilegia chrysantha* var. *rydbergii.*

Hardiness Zones: 3 to 9

Bloom Time: late spring to early summer

Size: 2 to 3 feet tall and wide

Sun: Full to part shade

Water: Average, well-drained

Butterfly Larval Host: Columbine duskywing butterfly

Wildlife Food Value: Hummingbirds, long-tongued bees

Aquilegia chrysantha has striking golden blooms.

Colorado Blue Columbine

Aquilegia caerulea

Description: Colorado Blue Columbine is known for its lively blue flowers. The flowers' long spurs contain nectar that hummingbirds can access with their long tongues. Native to western North America.

Hardiness Zones: 3 to 10

Bloom Time: April to May

Size: 1 to 2 feet tall and wide

Sun: Full to part shade

Water: Average

Butterfly Larval Host: Columbine Duskywing butterfly

Wildlife Food Value: Hummingbirds, long-tongued bees (bumblebees are the primary visitors)

These flowers are mainly visited by bumblebees.

Coreopsis Plants

Family: Asteraceae (daisy family); Genus: *Coreopsis*

Description: Coreopsis is commonly known as tickseed because its seeds are small, dark, and relatively flat, resembling ticks. I've included perennial tickseed plants; you can also consider several re-seeding annuals for your pollinator garden. Through hybridization and breeding programs, cultivars that showcase shades of red have been introduced.

Coreopsis verticillata has bright blooms and fine foliage.

California Tickseed

Coreopsis douglasii

Description: While California tickseed is an annual, if left to go to seed, it can readily self-seed for new plants the following year. Sporting yellow centers and rays, with fleshy foliage found mainly at the base of the plant. Native to California.

Hardiness Zones: 2 to 11

Bloom Time: May to July

Size: 10 inches tall by 1 to 2½ feet wide

Sun: Full

Water: Dry to average

Butterfly Larval Host: Silvery checkerspots

Wildlife Food Value: Butterflies, short- and long-tongued bees

The common name "tickseed" refers to the shape of the seed, which resembles a tick.

Threadleaf Tickseed, Whorled Coreopsis

Coreopsis verticillata

Description: Threadleaf tickseed has lovely, profuse, and long-lasting yellow daisy-like flower heads with yellow centers and rays, spreading by rhizomes. It is also known for its fine, threadlike foliage. Threadleaf grows erect and in clumps with multiple stems. Native to the eastern United States.

Hardiness Zones: 3 to 9

Bloom Time: June to September

Size: 2 to 3 feet tall by 1½ to 2 feet wide

Sun: Full

Water: Dry to average

Butterfly Larval Host: Buckeye and silvery checkerspot

Wildlife Food Value: Butterflies, short- and long-tongued bees

Coreopsis verticillata blooms throughout the summer.

Large-Flowered Tickseed

Coreopsis grandiflora

Description: A summertime showstopper, known for its large, vibrant yellow flowerheads—up to three inches wide. There are cultivars with red at the base of the flower's rays. Native to eastern North America.

Hardiness Zones: 4 to 9

Bloom Time: June to August

Size: 1½ to 2½ feet tall by 1 to 1½ feet wide

Sun: Full

Water: Dry to average

Butterfly Larval Host: No butterflies, some moths

Wildlife Food Value: Butterflies, short- and long-tongued bees

The large-flowered tickseed has brilliant yellow blooms.

Lanceleaf Tickseed

Coreopsis lanceolata

Description: Bright yellow centers and rays, with lance-shaped foliage, give rise to the common name. Through re-seeding, lanceleaf tickseed will naturalize in your pollinator garden. Native to central and eastern North America.

Hardiness Zones: 4 to 9

Bloom Time: May to July

Size: 1 to 2 feet tall by 1 to 1½ feet wide

Sun: Full

Water: Average

Butterfly Larval Host: Silvery checkerspot

Wildlife Food Value: Butterflies, short- and long-tongued bees

Coreopsis lanceolata often grows in clusters.

Crossvine

Bignonia capreolata

Description: There are about 28 species of Bignonia and only one crossvine native to the US, from northeastern, north-central, south-central, and southeastern regions, ranging from southern Ontario to Florida and west to Texas and Illinois. The remainder are found in the tropical areas of South America. I'm thankful for the one we have. I have two in the Bee Better Teaching Garden: one over an arbor and another trellising from a tall tree. They put on a spectacular display each spring. Our native crossvine is a vigorous, semi-evergreen, perennial vine. The common name arises when a cross-section of its stem reveals the wood forming a cross. Four distinct bands of phloem form the cross-shaped pattern.

Hardiness Zones: 5 to 9

Bloom Time: Early spring

Size: 35 feet tall and 50 feet wide

Sun: Full to partial shade

Water: Average

Butterfly Larval Host: Gray hairstreak butterfly

Wildlife Food Value: Butterflies, hummingbirds, short- and long-tongued bees

One of the beloved crossvines in my Bee Better Teaching Garden.

Cup Plants

Family: Asteraceae (daisy family); Genus: Silphium

Description: A deep-rooted, drought-tolerant perennial prairie plant, cup plants thrive in pollinator gardens if they are within your hardiness zone and average moisture. The genus is tall, so siting one or several in your garden needs careful thought. In the past, I've underestimated the height of the cup plant, *Silphium perfoliatum*, but found that in the fall, it transplanted easily, even with the deep roots, but I had to dig deep. Cup plants are so named because the upper leaves surround the stem to form a cup-like structure that holds water after a rain. The collected water makes it a water source, although temporary, for birds and other wildlife. Another common name for *Silphium* spp. is rosinweed, due to the excretion of a resinous sap from the stems when broken.

Cup plants are drought tolerant but very tall—carefully plan their placement.

Compass Plant

Silphium laciniatum

Description: Oh, she's a big one! Compass plants, with their yellow, sunflower-like flower heads, often survive decades. The common name has an interesting story. The plant is characterized by its distinctive deeply lobed leaves, which often orient north-south, hence the name. Native to the eastern and central United States, extending as far west as New Mexico.

Hardiness Zones: 3 to 8

Bloom Time: July to September

Size: 5 to 9 feet tall by 1½ to 3 feet wide

Sun: Full

Water: Average

Butterfly Larval Host: No butterflies, some moths

Wildlife Food Value: Butterflies, hummingbirds, short- and long-tongued bees

Compass plants can be very long-lived.

Cup Plant

Silphium perfoliatum

Description: Plant in the back of the border. The common name comes from the triangular to ovate leaves surrounding the stem, which appear like a cup-like vessel. While it will hold water after a rain, I wouldn't consider it a water source. Three-inch flower heads are light yellow with a darker yellow center disk. Native to the central to eastern United States and Canada.

Hardiness Zones: 3 to 9

Size: 4 to 8 feet tall and 1 to 3 feet wide.

Sun: Full

Water: Average to wet

Butterfly Larval Host: Silvery checkerspot, Gorgone checkerspot, bordered patch, painted lady butterfly

Wildlife Food Value: Butterflies, hummingbirds, short- and long-tongued bees

These blooms can reach up to three inches wide.

Starry Rosinweed

Silphium asteriscus

Description: Large, bright lemon-yellow colored flower heads, surrounded by a center of yellow to green disk florets, bloom in late summer. A robust wildflower occurs naturally in flatwoods, sandy pinelands, and disturbed areas. The name rosinweed comes from the resinous sap, which, when dried, was used by Native Americans as a breath-freshening chewing gum. Native to central and eastern North America.

Hardiness Zones: 4 to 8

Bloom Time: June to September

Size: 2 to 5 feet tall and 1½ to 3 feet wide

Sun: Full to part shade

Water: Drought tolerant once established

Butterfly Larval Host: No butterflies, some moths

Wildlife Food Value: Butterflies, hummingbirds, short- and long-tongued bees

Silphium asteriscus is a food source for many butterflies, hummingbirds, and bees.

Rosinweed

Silphium integrifolium

Description: One difference between the commonly named rosinweed, *Silphium integrifolium*, and starry rosinweed, *Silphium integrifolium*, is their height. Rosinweed is taller and can grow up to 6 feet high, while starry rosinweed is shorter, only reaching 2 to 5 feet in height. However, the difference doesn't stop there; other differences can be found in leaf arrangement. Rosinweed has opposite leaves with smooth, toothless leaf edges. Starry rosinweed leaves are generally alternate, with rough, hairy, and toothed edges. Native to the central US

Hardiness Zones: 4 to 8

Bloom Time: July to September

Size: 2 to 6 feet tall by 1 to 3 feet wide

Sun: Full

Water: Average

Butterfly Larval Host: No butterflies, some moths

Wildlife Food Value: Butterflies, hummingbirds, short- and long-tongued bees

Rosinweed is taller than starry rosinweed.

Joe-Pye Weeds

Family: Asteraceae (daisy family); Genus: *Eutrochium*

Description: Most Eutrochiums are tall, and maybe too tall for a small garden. You may want to look for one of the many shorter cultivars. Another genus name change was made, from *Eutrochium* to *Eupatorium*. Many nurseries still list Joe-Pye weeds as *Eupatorium*. Both are acceptable, though. Scientific references will use *Eupatorium*, and if you are as dyslexic as I am, they look the same! The five recognized species are listed below. The reference to the common name, Joe-Pye weed, has a great story behind it. The story centers around a Mohican *sachem* ("tribal chief"), most likely Joseph Shauquethqueat, who was known to his white neighbors in Massachusetts as Joe Pye. Native Americans were known to use Joe-Pye weed to treat fevers, dysentery, and kidney problems.

A monarch butterfly nectaring at a Joe-pye weed.

Hollow Joe-Pye Weed

Eutrochium fistulosum

Description: Large, compound inflorescences composed of many tiny, vanilla-scented flowers. A tall Joe-pye weed with hollow stems. I particularly like this one because its hollow stems are often used as nesting sites for mason and leafcutter bees. If cutting back, be sure to leave at least 6 to 8 inches to provide nesting sites. Native to the central and eastern United States and Ontario.

Hardiness Zones: 4 to 8

Bloom Time: July to September

Size: 4 to 7 feet tall and 2 to 4 feet wide

Sun: Full to partial shade

Water: Average to wet

Larval Host: Pearl crescent butterfly

Wildlife Food Value: Butterflies, hummingbirds, long-tongued bees

These plants provide nectar for butterflies and hummingbirds, but they're also nesting sites for many types of bees.

Spotted Joe-Pye Weed

Eutrochium maculatum

Description: A beautiful, but very tall Joe-Pye weed, the stems of spotted Joe-Pye weed are striking, with purple-spotted or purple stems and whorled leaves. I grow it at the back of my mixed border, where height is welcomed. Native to North America.

Hardiness Zones: 4 to 8

Bloom Time: July to September

Size: 4 to 7 feet tall by 3 to 4 feet wide

Sun: Full

Water: Average to wet

Butterfly Larval Host: Pearl crescent butterfly

Wildlife Food Value: Butterflies, hummingbirds, long-tongued bees

These plants are very tall—great backgrounds in in mixed borders or garden displays that need a little height.

Appalachian Joe-Pye Weed

Eutrochium steelei

Description: These are found exclusively in a specific geographic location and nowhere else on Earth—the Appalachian Mountains.

Hardiness Zones: 4 to 9

Bloom Time: July to September

Size: 6½ feet tall by 4 feet wide

Sun: Full to part shade

Water: Moist to wet

Butterfly Larval Host: Pearl crescent butterfly

Wildlife Food Value: Butterflies, hummingbirds, long-tongued bees

Appalachian Joe-pye weed growing in West Virginia.

Joe-Pye Weed, Sweet

Eutrochium purpureum

Description: A personal favorite of mine, growing in the waterwise transitional zone of the Bee Better Teaching Garden. Doug Tallamy lists Joe-pye weed as a highly valuable plant for native ecosystems, supporting a wide-range of insects, particularly butterflies. It's an essential late-season food source for pollinators seeking nectar and pollen. Native to the eastern and central US

Hardiness Zones: 4 to 9

Bloom Time: July to September

Size: 5 to 7 feet tall and 2 to 4 feet wide

Sun: Full to partial shade

Water: Average to wet

Butterfly Larval Host: Pearl crescent butterfly

Wildlife Food Value: Butterflies, hummingbirds, long-tongued bees

The eastern tiger swallowtail is just one of many butterfly species that benefit from sweet Joe-pye weed.

Lobelias

Family: Campanulaceae (bellflowers); Genus: Lobelia

Description: Two common Lobelia species are featured. Their distinct, two-lipped tubular flowers characterize *Lobelia* spp. While hummingbirds are the primarily pollinator, native bees, and honeybees also seek nectar; however, most bees cannot access the tiny tubular flowers, so they nectar-rob by poking a hole near the base where nectar is located.

A juvenile ruby-throated hummingbird feeding on a cardinal flower.

Cardinal Flower

Lobelia cardinalis

Description: Cardinal flowers add both color and verticality to the pollinator habitat. Be sure to plant it where you can sit back and enjoy the hummingbirds feasting and fighting over its scarlet blooms. It's a short-lived, clumping perennial spreading by reseeding and sending offshoots. Native to North America.

Hardiness Zones: 3 to 9

Bloom Time: July to September

Size: 2 to 4 feet tall by 1 to 2 feet wide

Sun: Full to part shade

Water: Average to moist

Butterfly Larval Host: No butterflies, some moths

Wildlife Food Value: Butterflies, hummingbirds, long-tongued bees

These bright red blooms are popular with butterflies, hummingbirds, and long-tongued bees.

Great Blue Lobelia

Lobelia siphilitica

Description: A native perennial pollinator plant known for its distinctive light to dark blue, tubular-shaped flowers with a two-lipped structure, the great blue lobelia has a clump-forming growth habit, thriving in moist to wet areas. It is short-lived but self-sowing. Native to the central and eastern US and Canada.

Hardiness Zones: 4 to 9

Bloom Time: July to September

Size: 2 to 3 feet tall by 1 to 1½ feet wide

Sun: Full

Water: Average moist, even moist clay

Butterfly Larval Host: No butterflies, some moths

Wildlife Food Value: Butterflies, hummingbirds, long-tongued bees (especially bumblebees)

Lobelia siphilitica does well in wetlands.

Lupines

Family Name: Lupines; Genus: Lupinus

Description: Lupines have pea-like blue to purple flowers and sometimes pink or white, arranged in terminal spikes—a cluster of flowers at the stem's ends, with palm-shaped foliage. This wild lupine is the only host plant for the endangered Kamer blue butterfly, native to the Great Lakes region.

Lupines have beautiful, spire-like clusters of flowers.

Lupine, Wild or Sundial

Lupinus perennis

Description: A perennial lupine, with elegant clusters of purple, pea-like flowers, on 1–2 foot stems. A beautiful pollinator plant in the garden and an absolutely stunning display when found in a field. Native to the western US and Canada.

Hardiness Zones: 3 to 8

Bloom Time: April through July

Size: 1 to 2½ feet tall and ½ to 1 foot wide

Sun: Full to part shade

Water: Moist, occasionally dry

Butterfly Larval Host: Clouded sulfur, eastern tailed blue, frosted elfin, gray hairstreak, Karner blue, Persius duskywing, silvery blue, wild indigo duskywing

Wildlife Food Value: Butterflies, hummingbirds, short- and long-tongued native bees, occasionally honeybees

Wild lupines host numerous varieties of butterfly larvae.

Lupine, Bluebonnet, Texas

Lupinus texensis

Description: Thriving in dry, sunny locations, the state flower of Texas and can be found growing on acres and acres. Erect stems are topped with clusters of 50 fragrant blue, pea-like flowers, with white tips. Native to Texas, Louisiana, Arkansas, and Oklahoma.

Hardiness Zones: 4 to 8

Bloom Time: April through May

Size: 1 to 2 feet tall and wide

Sun: Full

Water: Dry

Butterfly Larval Host: Eastern tailed-blues, gray hairstreak, and silvery blues

Wildlife Food Value: Butterflies, hummingbirds, long-tongued bees (especially bumblebees)

Lupinus texensis is popular with bumblebees.

Broadleaf Lupine

Lupinus latifolius

Description: A perennial pollinator plant characterized by showy spikes of blue, purple, or white pea-shaped flowers, broadleaf lupine thrives in various disturbed and low-fertility soils. Native to western North America.

Hardiness Zones: 4 to 9

Bloom Time: June through September

Size: 2 to 4 feet tall and wide

Sun: Full to part shade

Water: Average to moist

Butterfly Larval Host: Boisduval's blue, clouded sulfur, orange sulfur, Persius duskywing, and silvery blue

Wildlife Food Value: Butterflies, hummingbirds, long-tongued bees (especially bumblebees)

Like other lupines, broadleaf lupine is a host source for many species of butterfly.

Monardas

Family: Lamiaceae (mint family); Genus: Monarda

Description: Monarda is a genus of annual and herbaceous perennial plants native to North America. There are 25 recognized species, and I wish to grow them all. I've covered some of the most common species. The tubular-shaped flowers are hummingbird favorites, particularly red, but once in the garden, hummingbirds seek nectar from many different colors. Did you know bees cannot see the color red like we do? But bees will seek nectar from red monardas since they see ultraviolet light outside our vision. Bees' perception of color is based on wavelengths different from ours, perceiving red flowers as a light blend that guides them to nectar and pollen sources.

Monarda fistulosa is a plant commonly used for tea that is also beneficial to many pollinators.

Lemon Bee Balm

Monarda citriodora

Description: Lemon beebalm is an annual or sometimes a biennial wildflower native to the southern US and Mexico and characterized by its lemon-scented foliage. The flower stalks are stacked whorls of lavender, pink blooms, found in harsh landscapes—rocky or sandy prairies, pastures, and roadsides from South Carolina and Florida, and west to Texas. It is considered a self-seeding annual and will form large colonies in the right conditions. Traditionally, teas made from the leaves of lemon beebalm were used to treat respiratory ailments like colds and coughs.

Hardiness Zones: 2 to 11

Bloom Time: May through August

Size: 1 to 2½ feet tall by ¾ to 1 foot wide

Sun: Full to part shade

Water: Dry to average, well-drained soils

Butterfly Larval Host: No butterflies, some moths

Wildlife Food Value: Butterflies, hummingbirds, short- and long-tongued bees

Monarda citriodora is a self-seeding annual.

Bergamot, Wild Bee Balm

Monarda fistulosa

Description: An herbaceous perennial, it may be more familiar to you as an herbal tea, but it is also a pollinator magnet. It has fragrant foliage and sweet, light lavender, pink, or purple flowers. As a member of the mint family, it will naturalize in your garden. Feel free to divide it every two to three years. Native to North America.

Hardiness Zones: 3 to 8

Bloom Time: July through September

Size: 2 to 4 feet tall by 2 to 3 feet wide

Sun: Full to part shade

Water: Average

Butterfly Larval Host: No butterflies, some moths

Wildlife Food Value: Butterflies, hummingbirds, short- and long-tongued bees

Wild bee balm has fragrant foliage and blooms.

Dotted Bee Balm

Monarda punctata

Description: Another mint family favorite, bee balm forms alien-looking clumps, yellow with purple spots. Considered a short-lived, herbaceous perennial. As with most bee balm pollinator plants, it will re-seed profusely. Do not worry about unwanted clumps, pull, transplant, or share with friends—an adventurous and worthy naturalizer for your pollinator garden. Native to North America.

Hardiness Zones: 3 to 8

Bloom Time: June and July

Size: 1½ to 2 feet tall by ¾ to 1 foot wide

Sun: Full to part shade

Water: Dry to average

Butterfly Larval Host: No butterflies, some moths

Wildlife Food Value: Butterflies, hummingbirds, short- and long-tongued bees

Monarda punctata grows in lush clusters.

Scarlet Bee Balm

Monarda didyma

Description: A prolific spreader by self-seeding, scarlet bee balm will also spread by rhizomes to form colonies. It's easy to pull if it becomes too much, and it transplants well. Move it around your garden or share it with friends. Another tip: With a large clump, cut back by half the stalks before blooming, to extend the bloom time, while still providing flower nectar and pollen for pollinators. Native to the northeastern US and eastern Canada.

Hardiness Zones: 4 to 9

Bloom Time: June and July

Size: 2 to 4 feet tall by 2 to 3 feet wide

Sun: Full to part shade

Water: Average to wet

Butterfly Larval Host: No butterflies, some moths

Wildlife Food Value: Butterflies, hummingbirds, short- and long-tongued bees

Scarlet bee balm is prolific, but easily transplanted.

Mountain Mints

Family: Lamiaceae (mint family); Genus: Pycanthemum

Description: While most mountain mints are native to the eastern US and Canada, with the greatest species diversity in North Carolina, a California native species, *Pycanthemum californicum*, represents a westward extension of the genus's natural range. Mountain mints are a valued nectar source for pollinators.

Blunt mountain mint has a silvery color.

Virginia Mountain Mint

Pycnanthemum virginianum

Description: A strong, mint-like scent, narrow leaves, and dense clusters of white flowers characterize Virginia mountain mint. Native to the eastern US and into Canada.

Hardiness Zones: 3 to 7

Bloom Time: July to September

Size: 2 to 3 feet tall by 1 to 1½ feet wide

Sun: Full

Water: Average

Butterfly Larval Host: Gray hairstreak

Wildlife Food Value: Butterflies, hummingbirds, short- and long-tongued bees

Virginia mountain mint is a host plant for gray hairstreak larvae.

Blunt Mountain Mint

Pycnanthemum muticum

Description: Blunt mountain mint has lustrous oval leaves surrounding clusters of flowers that vary from white to purple. It emits a strong minty scent when the foliage is crushed. It will naturalize nicely in a border or woodland garden. Native to eastern US and into Canada.

Hardiness Zones: 4 to 8

Bloom Time: July to September

Size: 1 to 3 feet tall and wide

Sun: Full to part shade

Water: Average

Butterfly Larval Host: Gray hairstreak

Wildlife Food Value: Butterflies, hummingbirds, short- and long-tongued bees

Blunt mountain mint is a pollinator magnet, providing a rich nectar and pollen for bees, butterflies, wasps, and flies (such as the syrphid and tachinid flies).

Hoary Mountain Mint

Pycnanthemum incanum

Description: A vigorous grower spread by rhizomes, it is known for attracting pollinators. Its nectar-rich flowers particularly attract bees, butterflies, and hummingbirds. In late summer, small white to lavender-tinged flowers will emerge. Native to the eastern US and into Canada.

Hardiness Zones: 4 to 8

Bloom Time: July to September

Size: 2 to 3 feet tall by 3 to 4 feet wide

Sun: Full to part shade

Water: Dry to average

Butterfly Larval Host: No butterflies, some moths

Wildlife Food Value: Butterflies, hummingbirds, short- and long-tongued bees

Hoary mountain mint in the Blue Ridge Mountains of Virginia.

Narrow-Leafed Mountain Mint

Pycnanthemum tenuifolium

Description: Narrow-leafed mountain mint is prized for its delicate appearance, long-blooming season, and scented foliage. It is an erect, compact plant that branches to create a bushy look. White to pale lavender flowers form clusters of tiny, two-lipped blooms. Native to eastern and central North America.

Hardiness Zones: 4 to 8

Bloom Time: July to September

Size: 2 to 3 feet tall and wide

Sun: Full to part shade

Water: Dry to average

Butterfly Larval Host: Gray hairstreak

Wildlife Food Value: Butterflies, hummingbirds, short- and long-tongued bees

Narrow-leafed mountain mint has pale flowers.

Sierra or California Mountain Mint

Pycnanthemum californicum

Description: This mint grows in the mountains and foothills throughout California in chaparral, woodland, and forest. Small, densely packed flowers appear in white head-like clusters, with purplish or violet spots on the lower lip. Native to the Sierra Nevada, peninsular, eastern transverse, and inner northern California coast ranges.

Hardiness Zones: 7 to 10

Bloom Time: June to September

Size: 1 to 3 feet tall by 1 to 2 feet wide

Sun: Full to part shade

Water: Average to moist

Butterfly Larval Host: Gray hairstreak

Wildlife Food Value: Butterflies, hummingbirds, short- and long-tongued bees

California mountain mint at the California Botanic Garden in Claremont showing foliage as it looks before the clusters of flowers appear.

Penstemons

Family Name: Plantaginacea

Description: Most penstemons are perennial herbaceous plants with swollen nodes, but trees, shrubs, and vines are also present. The leaves of Plantaginacea family are simple, and arranged alternately on the stems. Each leaf has a peculiar pair of fused, sheathing stipules, known as an ochrea. Penstemons are native throughout the US, with the greatest number found in the western states.

A swallowtail butterfly visiting a Rocky Mountain penstemon.

Foothill Penstemon

Penstemon heterophyllus

Description: This perennial plant features charming white to pale pink, tubular flowers that resemble foxgloves. These attract butterflies, hummingbirds, various native bees such as bumblebees, sweat bees, leafcutter bees, and carpenter bees, as well as specialist bees like miner and mason bees, and honeybees. Native to California.

Hardiness Zones: 3 to 8

Size: 3 to 5 feet tall and 1½ to 2 feet wide

Sun: Full

Water: Moist to dry

Butterfly Larval Host: Baltimore checkerspot, variable checkerspot, Edith's checkerspot, and common buckeye

Wildlife Food Value: Butterflies, hummingbirds, short- and long-tongued bees

Foothill penstemon attracts many types of pollinators.

Large Beardtongue

Penstemon grandiflorus

Description: Large-flowering perennial with light lavender to bluish-purple flowers, this handsome plant provides nectar or pollen for each of our four featured pollination groups. Tubular-shaped flowers are arranged horizontally and are prolific. Long ago, Native Americans treated toothaches by chewing on the root pulp. Native to the central US

Hardiness Zones: 3 to 8

Bloom Time: May to June

Size: 2 to 4 feet tall by 1 to 1½ feet wide

Sun: Full, part shade

Water: Dry, average, drought-tolerant, well-drained

Butterfly Larval Host: Baltimore, variable, Edith's checkerspots, and the common buckeye

Wildlife Food Value: Butterflies, hummingbirds, short- and long-tongued bees

Penstemon grandiflorus is a good food source for bumblebees.

Venus Penstemon

Penstemon venustus

Description: A long-lived herbaceous to woody subshrub, Venus penstemon (also known as Alpine penstemon) is characterized by its showy, tubular-shaped, lavender to purple flowers. With a strong taproot, the Venus penstemon is drought-tolerant once established. It grows in open areas and has rocky outcroppings in the high Cascades along the Columbia River Gorge. Cultivates well in a rock garden. Venus penstemon is a crucial nectar source for hummingbirds and butterflies. Bumblebees access nectar through nectar-robbing. Native to the northwestern US

Hardiness Zones: 4 to 8

Bloom Time: May to August

Size: 1 to 3 feet tall by 1½ feet wide

Sun: Full

Water: Dry, average, well-drained

Butterfly Larval Host: Common buckeye, variable checkerspot, and Edith's checkerspot.

Wildlife Food Value: Butterflies, hummingbirds, short- and long-tongued bees

Venus penstemon do well in rock gardens.

Firecracker Penstemon

Penstemon eatonii

Description: Firecracker penstemon is a drought-tolerant perennial that requires minimal watering once established. It is a hummingbird favorite and a striking perennial characterized by evocative, large, bright red, tubular flowers in spring through summer. This heat-loving pollinator plant is often used in desert landscapes and rock gardens. Native to the southwestern US

Hardiness Zones: 4 to 8

Bloom Time: May through August

Size: 2 to 3 feet tall by 1 to 2 feet wide

Sun: Full

Water: Dry

Butterfly Larval Host: Various checkerspots and common buckeye

Wildlife Food Value: Butterflies, hummingbirds, short- and long-tongued bees

Hummingbirds are attracted to firecracker penstemon.

Hairy Beardtongue

Penstemon hirsutus

Description: The species name, *hirsutus*, is the Latin word for hairy, shaggy, or bristly. Think Bigfoot! This is a tall perennial with hairy stems and upright growth, with stalked clusters of lavender to violet trumpet-shaped flowers with lips of white. Native to eastern North America.

Hardiness Zones: 3 to 9

Bloom Time: May through June

Size: 1 to 2 feet tall and ½ to 1½ feet wide

Sun: Full

Water: Dry to medium

Butterfly Larval Host: Common buckeye and Baltimore checkerspot

Wildlife Food Value: Butterflies, hummingbirds, short- and long-tongued bees

Penstemon heterophyllus has bright shades of blue and purple.

Phlox

Family: Polemoniaceae (phlox or Jacob's Ladder)

Description: I shouldn't name favorites in my pollinator habitat, but phlox is a fave, right under Joe-Pye weeds. Phlox are characterized by their five-merous flowers (meaning they have parts in multiples of five), with petals often fused into a salverform or bell-shaped corolla. There has been extensive breeding of phlox; in essence, phlox breeding has dramatically diversified the options available to gardeners, offering a wider array of colors, forms, sizes, and improved disease resistance and adaptability to various growing conditions. There are numerous cultivars to choose from, allowing for planting in most garden conditions. Four phlox species include spring-blooming plants—*P. subulata*, called moss phlox; *P. stolonifera*, or creeping phlox; *P. divaricata*, commonly referred to as wild blue phlox, woodland phlox, wild blue phlox, or wild sweet William, and the summer-flowering. *P. paniculata*, garden phlox. My focus in my home garden is growing *P. divaricata* and as many new *P. paniculata* I can find. There are lots of different ones. I'm a wanna be collector.

Garden phlox is a favorite among pollinator gardens, especially those who enjoy a cottage garden style.

Wild Sweet William

Phlox divaricata

Description: An apt common name for *Phlox divaricata* is wild sweet William. It's a low-growing phlox with an abundance of bluish, five-petal flowers with an open face. Also known as woodland phlox, it grows in rich woodlands, fields, and along creeks. Native to eastern North America.

Hardiness Zones: 3 to 8

Bloom Time: April to May

Size: ¾ to 1 foot tall and wide

Sun: Full to part shade

Water: Average

Butterfly Larval Host: No butterflies, some moths

Wildlife Food Value: Butterflies, hummingbirds, short- and long-tongued bees

Wild sweet William is often found in woodlands and along creeks.

Moss Phlox

Phlox subulata

Description: The common name for *Phlox subulata* is moss phlox, due to its clumping form resembling acrocarpous mosses. It grows into a creeping mat that will delightfully spill over a retaining wall or flow over the concrete if planted next to a driveway or path. Native to eastern and central US

Hardiness Zones: 3 to 9

Bloom Time: March to May

Size: ¼ to ½ feet high by 1 to 2 feet wide

Sun: Full

Water: Average

Butterfly Larval Host: No butterflies, some moths

Wildlife Food Value: Butterflies, hummingbirds, long-tongued bees

Moss phlox creates attractive moss-like clumps of flowers.

Creeping Phlox

Phlox stolonifera

Hardiness Zones: 5 to 9

Description: Creeping phlox forms a lovely, loose mat of semi-evergreen foliage, with erect lavender, blue, or white flowers with a purple-red tinged eye. As the species suggests, stolonifera has two types of above-ground stems: low leafy stolons, and flowering stems that rise above the foliage. Native to southeastern US

Bloom Time: July to September

Size: ½ to 1 feet tall and ¾ to 1½ feet wide

Sun: Full to part shade

Water: Average

Butterfly Larval Host: No butterflies, some moths

Wildlife Food Value: Butterflies, hummingbirds, short- and long-tongued bees

The 'Sherwood Purple' cultivar demonstrates the two types of stems you'll see on creeping phlox.

Garden Phlox

Phlox paniculata

Hardiness Zones: 4 to 8

Description: Commonly referred to as garden phlox, (as in every garden should include it if it's in the right hardiness zone). It's loved by hummingbirds and butterflies, with the bonus of gold finches feeding on the seed. The colors range from pink and purple to white, and cultivars offer a wider range of colors. Garden phlox is prone to powdery mildew, so look for resistant cultivars such as 'David' (White) or 'Jeana' (Purple). Native to the eastern US

Hardiness Zones: 4 to 8

Bloom Time: July to September

Size: 2 to 4 feet tall and 2 to 3 feet wide

Sun: Full, part shade

Water: Average

Butterfly Larval Host: No butterflies, some moths

Wildlife Food Value: Butterflies, hummingbirds, short- and long-tongued bees

Garden phlox is one of the most rewarding plants—benefiting an abundance of pollinators.

Phlox paniculata 'Jeana'—A Butterfly Crowd-Pleaser

As the mid-morning sun kisses blooming flowers in the mixed border, every flower type is visited by various pollinators, with the garden phlox, 'Jeana', receiving the most attention from butterflies.

Three 'Jeana' were planted initially eight years ago. Now, without counting, I see dozens. Phlox 'Jeana' spreads, but not aggressively. In optimal growing conditions, 'Jeana' will make itself at home. This fall, I'll transfer some of them to the back 40 feet to spread them out further.

This cultivar was discovered growing along the Harpeth River near Nashville, Tennessee, and named after its discoverer, Jeana Prewitt. Standing five feet tall, this lavender-colored beauty produces an impressive floral display from mid-July through early September, during the times when butterfly activity is at its highest. While not considered the showiest phlox as a flower form, in my mind, 'Jeana' is the showiest of all when covered with a variety of butterflies.

The Trial Garden of Mt. Cuba Center in Delaware conducted phlox trials between 2015 and 2017, revealing phlox paniculata 'Jeana' to be the best of the best on many factors, including resistance to powdery mildew and butterfly activity by a large margin. Although still unproven, the idea is that 'Jeana' is preferable because it allows butterflies to quickly access the nectar of many flowers without moving as frequently.

'Jeana' garden phlox is one of the best varieties of phlox to plant in a butterfly-friendly garden.

Rudbeckias

Family: Asteraceae (daisy family)

Description: There are many species of Rudbeckia, two of the most common and readily available in garden centers—orange coneflower, *Rudbeckia fulgida*, and black-eyed Susans, *Rudbeckia hirta*. I've detailed others worth trying to find in garden centers or growing from seed. They are great plants! The specialist native bee, *Andrena rudbeckiae*, focuses on rudbeckia. The genus is named for Olof Rudbeckia, a Swedish botanist who lived from 1630 to 1702 and founded the Uppsala Botanic Garden, where Carl Linnaeus was a professor of botany.

A common buckeye butterfly nectaring from a black-eyed Susan.

Black-Eyed Susan

Rudbeckia hirta

Description: A bright-eyed, yellow-glowing, earthy-looking pollinator plant, with 2 to 3 inch–wide, daisy-like flowers with dark centers, hence the common name, black-eyed Susans. A short-lived perennial, bi-annual, or annual outside its hardiness range; worthy of growing for nectar, pollen, and as a butterfly host plant, even if only grown as an annual, but often self-seeds, or seeds can be directly sown after the treat of the last frost date, and will bloom first year from seed. Native to the central US

Hardiness Zones: 3 to 7

Bloom Time: June to September

Size: 2 to 3 feet tall and 1 to 2 feet wide

Sun: Full

Water: Average, drought-tolerant once established

Butterfly Larval Host: bordered patch, Gorgone checkerspot, and silvery checkerspot

Wildlife Food Value: Butterflies, hummingbirds, short- and long-tongued bees

Black-eyed Susans may self-seed, but can also be directly sown right after the last frost date.

Cutleaf Coneflower

Rudbeckia laciniata

Description: Watch this one; she is a spreader! Some readers are looking beyond their home garden and are looking for spreaders, perhaps creating a prairie or community garden with space. This Rudbeckia is for you. I grow it in my home garden in the back 40 feet, with lots of room to spread. I also share it with like-minded friends. In the wild, cutleaf coneflower will reach up to 9 feet tall. Reportedly, in a cultivated garden, it has a shorter stature, typically growing 3 to 4 feet tall. Mine in Raleigh is somewhere in between. It's a great plant if you have room for it. Native to North America.

Hardiness Zones: 3 to 9

Bloom Time: July to September

Size: 2 to 9 feet tall by 1½ to 3 feet wide

Sun: Full to part shade

Water: Average

Butterfly Larval Host: Bordered patch, gorgone checkerspot, and silvery checkerspot

Wildlife Food Value: Butterflies, hummingbirds, short- and long-tongued bees

Rudbeckia laciniata is a great option if you have a large amount of space to fill out in your garden.

Orange Coneflower or Black-Eyed Susan

Rudbeckia fulgida

Description: Rudbeckias perform best in full sun but will tolerate some light shade—a perennial plant with bright yellow-orange daisy-like flowers and a prominent dark brown cone in the center. Although cultivars aren't explicitly addressed in this book, I would be remiss if I didn't mention the widely available *Rudbeckia fulgida* var. *sullivantii* 'Goldsturm'. Native to the southeastern US

Hardiness Zones: 3 to 9

Bloom Time: July to August

Size: 2 to 3 feet tall by 2 to 2½ feet wide

Sun: Full

Water: Dry to average

Butterfly Larval Host: Bordered patch, Gorgone checkerspot, and silvery checkerspot

Wildlife Food Value: Butterflies, hummingbirds, short- and long-tongued bees

Butterflies, hummingbirds, and bees all benefit from orange coneflowers in a garden.

Western Coneflower

Rudbeckia occidentalis

Description: What a funky flower! OK, well, interesting is a better word. This Rudbeckia is unusual in that it lacks the usual yellow petals around its dark-brown flower heads. Considered an excellent pollinator plant for butterflies and bees. Native to northwestern US

Hardiness Zones: 3 to 9

Bloom Time: July to October

Size: 3 to 5 feet by 1½ to 2 feet wide

Sun: Full

Water: Average to moist

Butterfly Larval Host: No butterflies, some moths

Wildlife Food Value: Butterflies, hummingbirds, short- and long-tongued bees

Western coneflowers require direct sunlight.

Brown-Eyed Susan

Rudbeckia triloba

Description: Brown-eyed Susan is a native wildflower that thrives in cultivated gardens with full sun and well-drained soil. It's a cheerful and important pollinator addition to your fall garden, especially for butterflies and bees. Native to central-eastern US

Hardiness Zones: 4 to 8

Bloom Time: July to October

Size: 2 to 3 feet tall by 1 to 1½ feet wide

Sun: Full

Water: Average

Butterfly Larval Host: Bordered patch, Gorgone checkerspot, and silvery checkerspot

Wildlife Food Value: Butterflies, hummingbirds, short- and long-tongued bees

Rudbeckia triloba blooms summer through early fall.

Large Coneflower

Rudbeckia maxima

Description: The flowers have prominent, dark brown center cones, surrounded by yellow rays. A delightful surprise for the pollinator garden. It's a tall, striking perennial for the back of the border. Native to the central and southern US

Hardiness Zones: 4 to 9

Bloom Time: June to July

Size: 5 to 7 feet tall by 3 to 4 feet wide

Sun: Full

Water: Dry to average

Butterfly Larval Host: Bordered patch and silvery checkerspot

Wildlife Food Value: Butterflies, hummingbirds, short- and long-tongued bees

Rudbeckia maxima can reach heights up to 7 feet, so it's best used as a background in borders.

Salvias

Family: Lamiaceae (mint family)

You'll often hear salvias commonly referred to as sage—the common English name for salvia, likely derived from the French word *sauge* for the herb, which was also associated with its healing qualities. The English specifically referred to the culinary herb *Salvia officinalis*, native to the Mediterranean and the Middle East.

A female swallowtail butterfly (black form) on blue sage.

Blue Sage

Salvia azurea

Description: Oh, that blue! Cut back plant stems by up to half in late spring to promote compactness and to prevent flopping. Repeat bloomers from summer until frost, regular moisture will encourage more blooms. Remove spent flower spikes to help extend the bloom period. Native to the southeastern US

Hardiness Zones: 5 to 9

Bloom Time: July to October

Size: 3 to 5 feet tall by 2 to 4 feet wide

Sun: Full

Water: Dry, average

Butterfly Larval Host: No butterflies, some moths

Wildlife Food Value: Butterflies, hummingbirds, short- and long-tongued bees

Given the right circumstances, blue sage will bloom repeatedly throughout the flowering season.

Black Sage

Salvia mellifera

Description: Fragrant evergreen shrub found in coastal sage scrub and chaparral habitats. A hardy, drought-tolerant shrub. It will thrive in a cultivated garden but give it a lot of room as it is a very large pollinating shrub. Great for Mediterranean-style gardens. Native to California and Baja California, Mexico.

Hardiness Zones: 7 to 10

Bloom Time: April to July

Size: 3 to 6 feet tall and 3 to 10 feet wide

Sun: Full

Water: Dry

Butterfly Larval Host: No butterflies, some moths

Wildlife Food Value: Butterflies, hummingbirds, short- and long-tongued bees

Black sage is a hardy plant, native to the drier spaces of California.

Mealycup Sage

Salvia farinacea

Description: A shrubby, clump-forming, short-lived perennial with a powdery or mealy appearance of the flower bracts. The cup reference is because of the shape of the calyx. The violet-blue flowers are enchanting. There are cultivars in white or purple. Native to the south-central US and northeast Mexico.

Hardiness Zones: 8 to 10

Bloom Time: May to frost

Size: 1 to 3 feet tall by 1 to 2 feet wide

Sun: Full to part shade

Water: Average, well-drained

Butterfly Larval Host: No butterflies, some moths

Wildlife Food Value: Butterflies, hummingbirds, short- and long-tongued bees

Butterflies, hummingbirds, and short- and long-tongued bees are all attracted to mealycup sage.

Hummingbird Sage

Salvia spathacea

Description: Magenta-colored flower spikes delight California beachcombers and work well in a cultivated garden, provided the culture needs listed below are met—a hummingbird favorite, spreading by rhizomes, forming a groundcover for dry areas. Native to California.

Hardiness Zones: 8 to 11

Bloom Time: March through May

Size: 1 to 3 feet tall by 3 feet wide

Sun: Full to part shade

Water: Dry; drought-tolerant once established

Butterfly Larval Host: No butterflies, some moths

Wildlife Food Value: Butterflies, hummingbirds, short- and long-tongued bees

Salvia spathacea is, of course, a favorite of hummingbirds. It also attracts butterflies and bees.

Solidagos

Family: Asteraceae (daisy family)

Solidagos produce bright, yellow fall blooms in dense clusters on the top of tall stems, featuring characteristic daisy-like flowers. There are 120 species and many cultivars. Among them, goldenrods are prolific nectar and pollen producers. This long-lasting fall bloomer is particularly important for its 11 specialist native bees. Deadhead them to extend the flowering cycle. Solidagos will naturalize in your garden, so give it space or divide every two or three years to control its spread. It is an important fall nectar and pollen-rich perennial—a personal favorite of mine—and a critical nectar source for southbound migrating monarchs. Many shy away from goldenrods because they are often confused with the ragweed, *Ambrosia artemisiifolia*, a common allergen. But goldenrod is a keystone species, playing a critical role in our ecosystem. Plant it for your fluttering friends!

Goldenrods are one of the most important late-blooming flowers for pollen and nectar, especially for those pollinators preparing to migrate or hibernate.

Giant Goldenrod

Solidago gigantea

Description: A tall, rhizomatous goldenrod, native to North America, provides a nectar- and pollen-rich source for late-blooming pollinators. Another spreader, so let this herbaceous perennial do so! Goldenrods are an underused pollinator plant. As the name suggests, giant goldenrod is tall, so place in the back of the border. Native to North America.

Hardiness Zones: 3 to 8

Bloom Time: August to September

Size: 3 to 7 feet tall and 2 to 6 feet wide

Sun: Full or part shade

Water: Average to wet

Butterfly Larval Host: Various checkerspots

Wildlife Food Value: Butterflies, hummingbirds, short- and long-tongued bees

Solidago gigantea is known as giant goldenrod or tall goldenrod.

Showy Goldenrod

Solidago speciosa

Description: Goldenrods, in general, are underappreciated, but it is not true of this showy and elegant goldenrod. Soft yellow, upright flowers on tall stems, show up loud and proud in your pollinator garden. I can't emphasize enough the importance of adding this keystone plant to your pollinator garden. **Native** to the central and eastern US

Hardiness Zones: 3 to 8

Bloom Time: July to September

Size: 2 to 3 feet tall and wide

Sun: Full

Water: Dry to average

Butterfly Larval Host: Various checkerspots

Wildlife Food Value: Butterflies, hummingbirds, short- and long-tongued bees

Showy goldenrod is an graceful plant that also has a lot of value for pollinators.

Canadian goldenrod

Solidago canadensis

Description: A showy goldenrod, but I love them all. Our native goldenrods are so vital to the fall pollinators, I would include them all, even if they were ugly ducklings! Wait, is there such a thing? Canadian goldenrod is native to North America, throughout Canada and the U. S., but not as far south as South Carolina, Georgia, Florida, Alabama, and Louisiana.

Hardiness Zones: 3 to 9

Bloom Time: August to October

Size: 4 to 5 feet tall and wide

Sun: Full

Water: Average

Butterfly Larval Host: Various checkerspots

Wildlife Food Value: Butterflies, hummingbirds, short- and long-tongued bees

Canadian goldenrod requires full sun and blooms from late summer through early fall.

California Solidago

Solidago californica

Description: If you are beginning to think that all goldenrods look the alike, you are not wrong! Clusters of small, ray florets are at the top of stems. Cluster sizes vary from 25 to several hundred flower heads. It will spread by rhizomes, so give her space to thrive, and share it with other pollinator habitat gardeners if it gets out of your bounds. Better yet, give to someone new to gardening to introduce them to this vital pollinator plant! **Native** to California.

Hardiness Zones: 6 to 10

Bloom Time: May through November

Size: 2 to 3 feet tall and wide

Sun: Full

Water: Dry, once established

Butterfly Larval Host: Various checkerspots

Wildlife Food Value: Butterflies, hummingbirds, short- and long-tongued bees

This isn't the showiest of goldenrods, but it is a keystone plant essential for local ecosystems.

Verbena

Family: Verbenaceae

Description: When you encounter a verbena in the Vervain family, Verbenaceae, you'll notice it has square stems, similar to those in the mint family. Other characteristics distinguish the two families, like flower structure and morphology. Most of the hundred or more species of Vervain are native to tropical regions of South America, Asia, and Europe, with the familiar common verbena, *Verbena officinalis*, native to England.

Plants in this family often have blue or purple flowers.

Blue Vervain

Verbena hastata

Description: Blue vervain is a long-legged, short-lived perennial addition that delights most pollinator gardeners. It can grow tall and happily dance above pollinator plants in your cultivated beds. Unusual, small flowers surround slender, branched spikes, thriving in wet areas. This old-fashioned plant is perfect for a cottage-style garden, and of course, in any pollinator garden, despite the style. **Native** to the eastern US and southern parts of Canada.

Hardiness Zones: 3 to 8

Size: 2 to 6 feet tall and 1 to 2½ feet wide

Sun: Full

Water: Average to wet

Butterfly Larval Host: Common buckeye

Wildlife Food Value: Butterflies, hummingbirds, long- and short-tongued bees, and some specialist bees

Blue vervain is often found in the wild in wetlands and near streambanks.

Rose Verbena

Glandularia canadensis

Description: Rose verbena, *Glandularia canadensis*, was formerly named *Verbena canadensis*. When purchasing plants, you may still find them under their previous name. Their colors vary from pink to magenta to rose-purple, but despite these variations, they are all lovely. Rose verbena is low-growing and spreads when the stem touches the ground, allowing it to root in. **Native** to eastern and south-central US

Hardiness Zones: 5 to 9

Bloom Time: May to August

Size: ½ to 1½ feet tall by 1 to 2 feet wide

Sun: Full

Water: Dry to average

Butterfly Larval Host: Common buckeye

Wildlife Food Value: Butterflies, hummingbirds, long-tongued bees

Rose verbena is a low-growing plant with beautiful purplish blooms.

Glossary

Acrocarpous mosses—Mosses having a tufted growth habit.

Apex—The tip or anterior cover of a butterfly's wing.

Caterpillar—*See larvae.*

Cheeses—The fruit of plants in the mallow family, *Malva spp.*, where the fruit is a disc-shaped capsule that breaks into seed-like segments, resembling a round of cheese.

Chevron—The V-shaped pattern or marking found on the wings of particular species, such as the red admiral butterfly.

Chrysalis—The form a caterpillar (larva) takes before it emerges from its cocoon as a fully formed butterfly (or moth), leaving behind its hard skin. For butterflies, the term used is specifically "chrysalis."

Corbicula—*See pollen baskets.*

Corolla tubes—The part of the flower formed when the petals fuse together, creating a tube-like structure that surrounds the reproductive organs.

Costa—The leading edge or front margin of the wing, extending from the wing's base to its apex.

Dimorphism, seasonal—Seasonal dimorphism represents two different forms. A phenomenon where a species exhibits different physical or behavioral traits depending on the time of year. For example, the eastern comma, *Polygonia comma*, has a smaller, darker winter form and a larger, paler summer form.

Dimorphism, sexual—Sexual dimorphism refers to the distinct differences in size or appearance between males and females. For example, the male eastern tiger swallowtail is always yellow, whereas the females can be either yellow or black.

Dorsal side—The upper surface of a butterfly's body and wings, visible when a butterfly holds its wings open.

Eclose—The moment when a butterfly emerges from its chrysalis.

Ecosystem—The ecosystem is all the biotic factors (living plants, animals, and microbes) and abiotic factors (nonliving elements like weather, Earth, sun, and soil) interacting with each other. Each organism has its own role in nature.

Eusociality—Common among bees, this refers to the highest level of social organization, exhibiting a reproductive division of labor, brood care, and overlapping generations.

Eyespots—Noticeable, round markings on the wings, featuring concentric rings of contrasting colors. These patterns are a form of mimicry that serves as a defense mechanism against predators since the eyespots resemble a vertebrate animal.

Family—A rank in the biological classification system to group similar genera based on shared evolutionary relationships and physical characteristics. From the broadest to the simplest, these classification ranks are Domain, Kingdom, Phylum, Class, Order, Family, Genus, and Species.

Forewing—Either of the two front wings of a four-winged insect.

Forewing undersides—The lower or ventral surface of the butterfly's forewings

Genera—Plural for genus.

Genus—In the taxonomic hierarchy, genus is placed between the family and species level. It is the first part of the organism's scientific name, always capitalized and italicized.

Gorget—The patch of colorful, iridescent feathers surrounding the neck of male hummingbirds.

Heterogametic—When females produce two types of eggs: those with a Z chromosome and those with a W chromosome. This plays a critical role in determining the sex of the offspring.

Hind margin—The rear edges of a butterfly's body part.

Hindwing—Either of the two back wings of a four-winged insect.

Hindwing undersides—The lower or ventral surface of the rear pair of a butterfly's hindwings.

Instar—The phase between two periods of molting. Most butterflies, but not all, go through five instars.

Larva—Also known as a caterpillar, where both words can be used interchangeably. Larva is the immature form of an insect, following the life cycle of egg, larva, chrysalis, and adult.

Larval host plant—A specific plant on which a butterfly (or moth) lays its eggs, whose leaves are eaten by the resulting larvae.

Marginal spot—A butterfly marking/pattern located in the marginal area, the region along the extreme outer edge of the wing.

Mimicking—The evolutionary adaptation where one butterfly species develops a resemblance to another to gain a survival advantage.

Monogametic—In which males produce only one type of sperm, each containing a Z chromosome.

Monolectic—Bees that collect pollen by specializing in a single plant species. An example is the sunflower leafcutter bee, *Megachile pugnata*.

Mudding—Where butterflies, typically males, engage in drinking from moist dung, ground dung, or mud, where they obtain salts and essential minerals not found in nectar. Also known as puddling.

Myrmecophily—A positive interaction between ants and other organisms, such as plants and insects, providing a symbiotic relationship.

Nectar-robbing—Nectar-robbing is when an insect or bird gets nectar from the base of the flower by creating a hole to sip nectar, sadly avoiding pollination. This behavior is often exhibited by bees that are too large to obtain nectar through conventional ways.

Oligolectic—Bees that collect pollen, specializing in a limited number of closely related flowering plant species. Examples of oligolectic bees are found in the bee families Andrenidae and Halictidae.

Osmeterium—A defensive organ found in swallowtail butterfly larvae.

Phenology—The study of the timing of seasonal events, such as blooming, leafing, migration, and hibernation.

Phloem—Plant tissue that transports sugars to leaves and other parts of the plant for growth or storage.

Pollen—The fine yellow powder produced by plants containing the male reproductive cells needed to fertilize the female part of the flower.

Pollen baskets—An arrangement of hairs found on the tibia of the hind legs of some bees. The bee collects pollen on its body hairs and then uses its legs to comb and pack it into these specialized baskets for easy transport back to the hive. Very common in bumblebees. Scientifically referred to as *corbicula*.

Polylectic—Generalist bees that collect pollen from diverse flowering sources. An example is the honeybee, *Apis mellifera*.

Puddling—Where butterflies, typically males, engage in drinking from moist dung, ground dung, or mud, where they obtain salts and essential minerals not found in nectar. Also known as mudding.

Scopa—A specialized pollen-carrying mechanism found on the body of most nonparasitic female bees, via a dense mass of hairs (setae) that are electrostatically charged to assist in pollen collection.

Setae—All bees have setae, the stiff, hair-like structures found on their bodies. Some bees have a more specialized setae, such as bumblebees, which have pollen baskets (corbicula), while others, like the mason bee, have setae on their abdomens to carry pollen.

Species—In the taxonomic hierarchy, species is placed after the genus level. It is the second part of the organism's scientific name, always italicized, but not capitalized.

Stolon—Creeping, horizontal plant stems or runners that set root, widening the plant's location.

Submarginal—The area or markings on the wing located near the wing's outer edge

Submarginal spots—A row of spots or a band of markings located in the submarginal area of the wings.

Thorax—The butterfly's middle body section, located between the head and the abdomen.

Ventral side—The underside of a butterfly that is visible when its wings are closed. The patterns create camouflage to hide the butterfly from predators while resting.

Indexes

Photo Credits

Key:FC = front cover, BC = back cover, t = top, m = middle, b = bottom, l = left, r = right

Unless otherwise noted, all photos are copyright Helen Yoest.
The following image is copyright Liz Condo: 196r
The following image is copyright Abby Levenson: 136
The following images are copyright Eric Carter: 11, 196l
The following images are copyright Nathalie Beauchamp: 54, 55
The following images are from Shutterstock.com: FCt: LedyX; FCm: Maria T Hoffman; FCbl, 181: Sheila Fitzgerald; FCbm, 21, 45, 183: Sundry Photography; FCbr, 24, 28bl, 28r, 34tr, 36, 41, 52, 53r, 57, 60, 75t, 77t, 83, 97, 102, 106, 119: Wirestock Creators; BC, 70: Eivor Kuchta; 3l, 9: Keith Hider; 3m, 66: Katie Dragon; 3r, 18t: Jevgenija ZUK; 6: rck_953; 7: Gordon Magee; 8t: debwhiteimages LLC; 8b: F.Neidl; 12t: 1000 Words; 12b: Ko Aun Lee; 14: contohdesainmyid; 15: Claudine Silaho Weber; 16t, 130, 154: tamu1500; 16m: Dmytro Lopatenko; 17: Iarisa Stefanjuk; 19: Martin Hibberd; 22: Yanyong Wongramphan; 23, 32b, 37, 56, 143, 144, 179: Kevin Collison; 25l, 25r: Nadya So; 26, 28tl, 146: Brian Woolman; 27t, 75b, 173: John A. Anderson; 27m: Kelsey Armstrong Creative; 27b: Sari ONeal; 29l, 29r, 35l, 35r: Jay Ondreicka; 30t, 92: Matt Cuda; 30b, 77b: SunflowerMomma; 31t: Chaizul; 31b: Kathryn White Photos; 32t: Jim and Lynne Weber; 33l, 33r: Larry Burk; 34l: The Image Party; 34br: Bonnie Taylor Barry; 39: gary powell; 43: Sheila Fitzgerald; 47: R.Moore; 49, 73, 76: vagabond54; 51: Petr Muckstein; 53l: Brandon Alms; 58: Stephan Morris; 59: chinahbzyg; 61: JamesChen; 62: meunierd; 63t: Wendy Riseborough; 63b: Riadi Pracipta66; 65: Luna343; 67, 68, 69: Nature's Charm; 71: Kris Wiktor; 72: Gregory Johnston; 74: Dennis W Donohue; 78, 94, 105: Victoria Virgona; 79t, 82b: thatmacroguy; 79b: Timelynx; 80: IJPhoto; 81t: Sue A Dunning; 81b: Freddi King; 82t: Slatan; 84: Gabi Wolf; 85: Roel Meijer; 87: media-ja; 88: Petr Ganaj; 90: Megan Kobe; 91: Mirko Graul; 95: Yuttana Joe; 98, 99: Paul Reeves Photography; 101: Nahidul Islam Sium; 103: D W Graves Photography; 107: Andi111; 108, 109: Jennifer Bosvert; 110: MaCross-Photography; 112: Danita Delimont; 113, 160, 162, 164: Susan Hodgson; 114: Lagutkin Alexey; 115: Tom Meaker; 116, 117, 155: Nahhana; 118: InfoFlowersPlants; 120: Mariusz S. Jurgielewicz; 121: Popova Valeriya; 122: DanushkaR; 123: Randy Bjorklund; 124: BGStock72; 125: Ted_USAJPN; 126, 149: APugach; 127: Jarod Quentin; 128, 138, 174: Kabar; 129: Svetlana Mahovskaya; 132, 134: weha; 133: TAMMY M JOHNSON; 135: Ahmed Noor Khan; 137: Jaclyn Vernace; 139: ahmydaria; 140: Malachi Jacobs; 141: Liz Albro Photography; 142: Patrick Jennings; 145: Drakuliren; 147: Sab.D; 148: Dixon Photography; 150: Salamanca1218; 151: Flower_Garden; 152: Donna Bollenbach; 153: Dajra; 157: Gerry Bishop; 158: John Ruberry; 161: Kazakov Maksim; 163: RukiMedia; 165, 189: ChWeiss; 166: MashimaraPhoto; 167: Aleksandra Duda; 168: katatonia82; 169: PAUL ATKINSON; 170: AJSTUDIO PHOTOGRAPHY; 171: TMNK Gardens; 172: Media Marketing; 175: AnnaRoth108; 176: Beekeepx; 177: SimoneHa; 178: meunierd; 180: guentermanaus; 182: Panumat Saenubon; 184: LifeCollectionPhotography; 185: Alex Manders; 186: Junoreda; 187: crystaldream; 188: Photography-by-Stretch; 190: Ziga13; 191: James Nature Pics

About the Author

Helen Yoest has lived in Raleigh, North Carolina since 1988. For the first ten years, she gardened on a tenth of an acre in an urban setting. Starting in 1998, her garden expanded to a half-acre in Raleigh's suburbs. Neither location is where one might expect to find an active and tidy pollinator habitat, but both gardens were, and are, full of life!

In addition to tending to her sustainable wildlife and pollinator habitat garden, Helen teaches classes in the garden on butterflies, birds, bees, and the native plants they favor. In addition, with a group of fabulous volunteers, she helps conserve the Joslin Garden in Raleigh.

www.BeeBetterNaturally.com

Acknowledgments

As an environmental scientist since 1985, I have extensive knowledge of the environment—air, soil, and water—my entire life's work has focused on improving the environment. Although I have gardened all my life, it wasn't until around 1988 that I redirected my focus toward wildlife gardening, particularly with a focus on pollinators.

Everything I know about pollinators today was self-taught, reading and attending lectures, and then giving lectures and classes. For fear of getting anything wrong herein, I asked the renowned University of Delaware professor, Dr. Douglas W. Tallamy, to review this book. Dr. Tallamy, who goes by Doug, advocates for a grassroots approach to conserving not only open land but also our home landscapes. Dr. Tallamy argues that declining wildlife populations are linked to the loss of our native plants. I couldn't agree more, and I have witnessed this firsthand over my decades as a wildlife habitat gardener. Doug's focus is on conservation and insects; my focus is on pollinators and the native plants that feed them. Doug is also the author of several books, including Nature's Best Hope. I hope you check it out. If there is an error in this book, it is mine and mine alone.

Friends have supported me along the way, in particular the Garden Girls—Aillene, Annie, Carol, Joanne, Ms. Ann, Nathalie, and Nell—and Don, the Garden Girls wannabe! Don and Nathalie help me keep my sanity; Joanne taught me ALWAYS to fact-check, even a copper penny. And Todd, who keeps me laughing! I have fact-checked until I was cross-eyed, so I sought additional help fact-checking from Nathalie Beauchamp and Karen Fitzmaurice.

But most of all, my daughter, Lily Philbrook, provided invaluable research that helped move the project along, and my husband, David, quietly listened as I reorganized the content of this book for the umpteenth time.